Improvised Adolescence

FOLKLORE STUDIES
IN A MULTICULTURAL
WORLD

The Folklore Studies in a Multicultural World series is a collaborative venture of the University of Illinois Press, the University Press of Mississippi, the University of Wisconsin Press, and the American Folklore Society, made possible by a generous grant from the Andrew W. Mellon Foundation. The series emphasizes the interdisciplinary and international nature of current folklore scholarship, documenting connections between communities and their cultural production. Series volumes highlight aspects of folklore studies such as world folk cultures, folk art and music, foodways, dance, African American and ethnic studies, gender and queer studies, and popular culture.

Improvised Adolescence

Somali Bantu Teenage Refugees in America

Sandra Grady

The University of Wisconsin Press

Publication of this volume has been made possible, in part, through support from the **Andrew W. Mellon Foundation**.

The University of Wisconsin Press
1930 Monroe Street, 3rd Floor
Madison, Wisconsin 53711-2059
uwpress.wisc.edu

3 Henrietta Street, Covent Garden
London WC2E 8LU, United Kingdom
eurospanbookstore.com

Printed in the United States of America

Library of Congress Cataloging-in-Publication Data

Grady, Sandra, author.
Improvised adolescence: Somali Bantu teenage refugees in America / Sandra Grady.
pages   cm — (Folklore studies in a multicultural world)
Includes index.
ISBN 978-0-299-30324-2 (pbk.: alk. paper)
ISBN 978-0-299-30323-5 (e-book)
1. Somalis—Cultural assimilation—United States.
2. Somalis—United States—Social life and customs.
3. Bantu-speaking peoples—Cultural assimilation—United States.
4. Somali American teenagers.   5. Refugees—Somalia.
6. Teenage refugees—United States.
I. Title.   II. Series: Folklore studies in a multicultural world.
E184.S67G73   2015
305.893´54073—dc23
2014030780

This work is dedicated to the memory of
Niall MacMenamin

I am because we are; we are because I am.

Contents

Illustrations

Preface

One day in the early 1990s, I found myself stuck in heavy traffic in Nairobi, Kenya, with two colleagues from Maria House, a facility in the Eastleigh area of the city engaged in empowering women from the surrounding slums through training in trades, a revolving loan fund, and a counseling and support program aimed at young women in crisis pregnancies. In the back seat of the car sat one of the longtime staff members, Peter Wainaina, probably in his late thirties at the time, who performed a variety of tasks in support of the program. Wainaina himself had only a few skills more than the women in our target population, but his knowledge of the vast Mathare Valley slum area that was the home of most of the students and some of the staff was invaluable to the program. Despite his lack of formal education, Wainaina was often a primary source of social and cultural information about the students and their daily lives. On this particular day, the city was crowded with out-of-town guests in preparation for a soccer match between Kenya's two largest ethnic groups, the Kikuyu and the Luo. As an outsider, my closest contact with this rivalry was what I learned in the news-paper, which was full of news about Parliamentary political factions splintering across ethnic lines. Because he had a captive audience in the car, Wainaina—himself a Kikuyu—began to explain to us that the match was high stakes. The Kikuyu, it seems, were required to beat the Luo, or they would be shamed before the rest of Kenya's citizens. The match ahead was critical, which was why the city was crowded with visitors from the rural areas.

Although I had no interest in soccer, the interethnic tensions that were causing political factionalism in Kenya had long been a puzzle to me. That year was the first in which parties outside of the ruling Kenya African National Union (KANU) party were able to form, but the rivalries between Kikuyu and Luo politicians had prevented any group from mounting a credible threat to KANU or President Moi, who had been in office for nearly a decade and a half at that point. Both ethnic groups had much to gain by forming a unity party, but the results so far had been disappointing. They could not agree on how to distribute leadership positions, so KANU remained dominant. In the midst of Wainaina's diatribe on the importance of beating the Luo in the weekend match, I attempted to learn more about politics. "Why does it matter so much?" I demanded, raising my voice a bit to interrupt his sports talk. "Why is it so important for the Kikuyu to beat the Luos?" His answer was surprising in its simplicity: "Because they are boys and not men," responded Wainaina, as if I had asked one of the most obvious questions he had ever received. "They are uncircumcised, and we are not, so we must beat them." Wainaina continued on, noting that because Luo men had not endured a rite of passage that involved the stoic endurance of pain, their victory would be humiliating to the Kikuyu. I stopped to gather my thoughts, because the answer was so unexpected. "Is this the same reason why they cannot agree to form a political alliance?" I asked. "The Kikuyu cannot share power with the uncircumcised?" Wainaina's response was matter of fact: "No Luo will ever be elected president of this country. We will not choose a boy to lead the nation."

I begin with this long-remembered bit of traffic conversation because it struck me forcefully that afternoon, and it changed how I came to think about ethnic rivalry. First, it highlighted the importance of something I had previously overlooked as a relatively unimportant cultural fact, that Kikuyu men circumcise and Luos do not in a rite of passage. Coming as I did from a culture where individual choices about circumcision had no repercussions in the larger political or sporting world, it opened a whole new way of thinking about the practice and its centrality to gender, ethnic, and age identity in East Africa. Before this conversation, I had assumed the rivalry between the two groups could be understood solely in terms of access to power or resources, and the inability to create a unified party had to do with sharing the two. But Wainaina's comment brought home the idea that some divisions may be more complicated than resource sharing and would be much more difficult for the average citizen, or *mwananchi*, to overcome when considering the nation's leadership.

The second thing that struck me was that something I imagined as private was completely public. Wainaina spoke to me in this matter-of-fact tone about something that was obvious, part of common knowledge. I was used to thinking of circumcision as an individual, private decision. I cannot remember ever having a conversation in a professional context with or about a male counterpart in which an individual's circumcision, or lack of one, was open for discussion. Nor have I ever heard it being an issue in political debate. Yet here it was revealed as a critical issue for judging a man's character and ability to lead.

Until then, it had not occurred to me how much intimate information was known about another person's body simply through ethnic affiliation and subsequent cultural practice, and that those practices—or lack of practice—were open for public opinion. Wainaina, who had never expressed any particular animosity toward other ethnic groups, who worked easily within the multiethnic staff at Maria House, did not bother to hide his disdain for uncircumcised men. If the disdain was as common as he indicated, it would have implications for the political life of the country far into the future.

In the twenty-odd years that have passed since that conversation, I have spent some time studying East African cultural practice and how it corresponds to ethnic identity. Nothing I have learned has led me to dismiss as idiosyncratic Wainaina's observations about the role of circumcision for marking ethnic superiority in the culture groups that practice it as a ritual of initiation. In fact, given the number of reported cases of forced circumcisions of Luos by Kikuyus during election violence in Kenya in 2007–8, circumcision remains an important identity marker. Consequently, when I learned of the large-scale resettlement of Somali Bantu refugees to the United States in 2004, a group coming from the rites of passage approach to the life course into U.S. models of adolescent education, my first question was how the group would integrate the cultural expectations of two sets of authority figures: traditional East African elders, and U.S. teachers and school administrators. So I set out to see how adolescence would unfold for these kids. What follows is the results of that research project.

Along the way, I had the support and assistance of a number of people. Gail DuPré and Chris Clements, at the Office of Migration and Refugee Services at the Archdiocese of Louisville, Kentucky, and Angela Plummer, the Director of Community Refugee and Immigration Services at the field site (which I cannot name by city because of research protocols that are detailed in the next chapter), provided early support of the project, which enabled me to make contacts within the Somali Bantu community in both locations. Brenda Custodio at the Municipal Schools was a crucial supporter of my research, while Saundra Brennan and Ken Woodard at the Municipal Schools provided approval for my research plans. Many faculty and staff members at the district welcome centers donated their time to help me learn about their students, but none were so generous as Sally Joslyn, Becky Lance, and Derrick Vickroy. It is difficult for research to happen without funding, and I want to thank the organizations who made this project possible through their financial support. The Blanton Owen Fund at the Library of Congress supported my initial research in Louisville, Kentucky, while the Dean of the Graduate Division of Arts and Sciences at the University of Pennsylvania supported my fieldwork, and the

American Association of University Women provided the financial support that allowed me to dedicate myself full time to writing the original draft. I am grateful to each organization for their belief in the value of my research. At various times in its development, this book has benefited from the insight and counsel of Dan Ben-Amos, Erika Brady, Simon Bronner, Lee Cassanelli, Christopher Dimmick, Mary Hufford, and Johanna Jacobsen Kiciman. The final version is a richer and more compelling work because of their ideas and encouragement. Sheila Leary at the University of Wisconsin Press has been a tireless advocate for the project, both with me and at the press. Her enthusiasm has never diminished, despite the demands of daily work that perpetually de-layed the submission of this manuscript. On a personal level, a number of people made the completion of this project possible. Julie Steelman Hall provided care to my aging father during my absences to conduct fieldwork, demonstrating such dedication and love that she became his favorite daughter and a permanent part of our family. I also want to thank Mary Frances Grady for her willingness to provide support while I juggled research with family obligations; I also must thank my parents, Thomas F. and Marjorie Grady, for their dedication to their children's education, as well as for their love and support throughout my life. I regret that I will not be able to share this book with them.

Finally, I want to thank the students and their families who participated in this study. Research protocols prevent me from thanking them by name, but I am grateful to each of them and their parents for their willingness to reveal and explain their lives to me. This research happened because the Somali Bantu community at Wedgewood welcomed me into their homes, classrooms, and lives with generosity and enthusiasm. I hope I have shared their stories respect-fully and well.

Improvised Adolescence

Introduction

The Somali Bantu

On a sunny day in late March in the midst of my fieldwork, the McGuffey Welcome Center celebrated the pending arrival of spring break by organizing a day-long field trip to a local skating arena for its students, a diverse population of teenage migrants and refugees from Latin America, Asia, and Africa. Displaced from their natal homes for a variety of often grievous reasons, these teenagers found themselves thrown together in an aging school building in the U.S. Midwest to learn English-language skills in a sheltered environment, rather than being mainstreamed into local high schools with comparatively limited English as a Second Language (ESL) resources. Most of the students had signed up to enjoy the skating trip, a diversion from their ordinary school routine, despite the five-dollar cost to participate in the event—a relatively high one for families with multiple students at the school and few resources.

Once at the rink, many of the students quickly strapped on their skates, and most of the Somali Bantu teenagers I had come to know through my research made their way toward and around the rink with varying degrees of proficiency. Hip-hop music blared from the speakers, providing an inescapable rhythm and attitude to the event. A few of the boys raced in and out on higher-status inline skates, moving to the beat and singing along to the lyrics as they weaved easily between fellow students of all nationalities. Obsiye, who was often in trouble with school authorities, was demonstrating his supreme fluency in hip-hop culture by singing and grooving to the music, and many of the boys suspected of being part of his gang were also skating effortlessly and confidently around the floor with little regard for the struggles of any of their classmates. Those Somali Bantu boys who were less enculturated into the gangsta lifestyle epitomized by hip-hop, like Mahdi, moved with less aplomb, but with great laughter, calling out to his friends and including them in the merriment of his successful movement forward on skates, however haphazard it was.

3

Tahlil (*right*) and a Somali Bantu classmate at a skating rink. Photo by author.

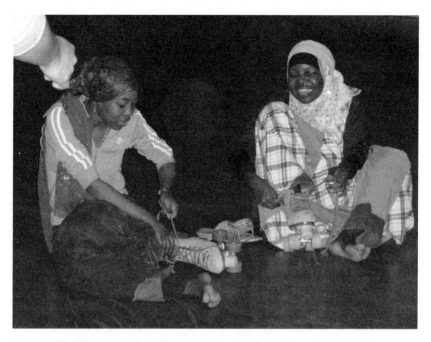

Timiro (*left*) and Maryan at a skating rink. Photo by author.

In contrast with the boys, most of the Somali Bantu girls were not initially successful as they moved about in their skates. They clustered in groups of two or three as they attempted not so much to move forward on skates but to simply keep the wheeled footwear from tangling in their floor-length skirts both on and off the rink. In this effort they had little success, and their ungraceful falls to the floor simply became part of the girls' experience of skating that bright, loud morning, as intrinsic as the successful maneuvers of their male counterparts. Hagarla tripped three times over her black lace underskirt before she agreed to lift it above her ankles and reveal the hems of the jeans she wore underneath. Fear of falling had prompted two of the girls, Maryan and Timiro, to pragmatically band together, each taking turns wearing a single pair of skates as the other walked beside her partner in shoes, keeping her upright. Despite this, the darting and weaving of the more proficient students was enough to disrupt them; they landed on the ground often, swapping skates for shoes each time.

In the background, the rink management announced repeated reminders to the kids to keep the flow of traffic moving properly on the floor through a public address system that could neither be heard above the music nor clearly understood by the students with their limited English skills. As some of the boys, like Ibraahin and Mahdi, gained skating proficiency, they busied themselves by offering shoulders and hands to support many of the girls circling the rink, taking advantage of the opportunity to be in close physical contact with girls of their own age and ethnicity. Most girls accepted them with enthusiasm, happy both to receive attention and to successfully move on wheels, if even for a short time, before the long skirts again hampered their progress. Dahabo and Haajiro, two fiercely independent girls, refused all offers of help from boys, while Afraxo found a quiet corner where she spent the bulk of the day sitting on the floor in her skates happily listening to Kenyan pop music on an iPod. As the day wore on, most of McGuffey's other students gave up skating for other rink activities, like pinball games, laser tag, and gossip, but most of the Somali Bantu kids continued to work at their proficiency in the rink. By the end, as students whirred by in brightly colored gangsta ensembles, or with their long skirts and sweaters eventually lifted and tied high enough about them to reveal jeans and logoed T-shirts as underlayers, the blur of movement, falls, laughter, and hip-hop music demonstrated the complex, multilayered, dizzying, and sometimes bruising experience of being a teenage Somali Bantu refugee attempting to re-settle in the U.S. Midwest.

It is this experience of teenagers in dizzying movement and their multiple layers that is the focus of this ethnographic study of young Somali Bantu refugees as they navigate adolescence in the United States. I selected this particular peer group not because their encounters with cultural adaptation are any more or less difficult than those of younger children or full-grown adult refugees but to explore the construct of adolescence as practiced by this population of dislocated agriculturalists in their initial efforts to adapt to American life. I want to note this limited focus from the beginning: this work is not meant to provide a comprehensive sketching of Somali Bantu expressive culture, nor is it meant to record how the community is currently practicing traditional initiation rituals in diaspora, nor is it a longitudinal study of a cohort over many years of adaptation to U.S. life. Rather, my aim is simpler here: to explore how a group of dislocated teens from an emerging culture group—along with their guardians and teachers—negotiate their passage into adulthood. This passage, a fundamental event in the traditional context that inculcates identity as adult, gendered members of the ethnic community, has been disrupted by their dislocation from East Africa and relocation to the United States. In this new environment of U.S. resettlement, these teens face different cultural expectations from the various authority figures they encounter. As a result, they are constructing adolescence in a unique and immediate moment of resettlement. These young people are an initiate group with a disrupted initiation; they have experienced a childhood in continuous flight, moving from the conflict zone of southern Somalia to life in a variety of refugee camps, and ultimately through resettlement to different cities in the United States. They are a generation raised entirely in diaspora. This work aims to look specifically at this unique set of agemates in this moment of cultural and developmental flux. One of the complex elements of identity formation for these kids stems from the emerging nature of the culture group itself, and to understand the development of these teens it is necessary to understand the emergence of the group as a single cultural identity.

Somali Bantu History and Identity

The name I have used so far for this group, Somali Bantu, is a recent one, adopted within international aid organizations to differentiate this population from their ethnic Somali counterparts, who also began to arrive in large numbers to refugee camps in northern Kenya soon after the collapse of the Somali state in 1991. The Somali Bantu category includes a number of ethnic minority groups who were marginalized by their history and labor within the Somali nation-state, and who lived in clusters of villages between the Jubba and Shebelle Rivers in southern Somalia prior to flight and resettlement. The word *Bantu* is not typically used to refer to a specific ethnic group, but is an overarching linguistic category that comprises a number of individual languages, just as *Romance* refers to French, Italian, and Spanish languages. In this case, the Bantu designation is a reference to the ancestral connection members of this group have with Africans from further south, but linguistically it is inappropriate, as their common language is not actually a Bantu one. Based on the linguistic evidence, most scholars accept that—perhaps a millennium ago—there was a proto-Bantu group, all speaking the same language, originating in central eastern Africa. Members of that group migrated out from a point of origin and, after centuries of migration and settlement, developed into differentiated linguistic (or ethnic) groups mostly in eastern, central, and southern Africa. The Gikuyu of central Kenya, the Swahili of the East African coast, and the Zulu of southern Africa are all examples of Bantu-speaking ethnic groups. By contrast, most members of the newly designated Somali Bantu community speak af-Maay (also called Maay-maay) as their primary language, which is a dialect of Somali, from the Cushitic language family. Current language use, however, obscures a complicated history that ties the group to a Bantu identity.

Amid the Bantu population migrations of the ninth to eleventh centuries, Bantu speakers settled into an area of present-day southern Somalia bordered by the Tana River, the Indian Ocean, and the Jubba and Shebelle Rivers, and they established a settlement at a place called Shungwaya. The Shungwaya settlement is both significant and controversial among historians. The earliest explorer-ethnographers to mainland East Africa failed to mention the existence of Shungwaya within the oral traditions of the people they encountered (Burton 1872, 67; Guillain 1856; Krapf and Ravenstein 1860), but subsequent nineteenth- and twentieth-century scholars found evidence of Shungwaya both in the *Kitub al-Zanj*, an Arabic manuscript of oral traditions, and within the contemporary stories of mainland peoples (Cerulli 1957; Grottanelli 1955; Prins 1950), so they accepted its existence as fact. By the 1970s Shungwaya had become a point of scholarly debate, with reconsiderations of the linguistic evidence and oral tradition (Morton 1972) and migration patterns (Turton 1975) leading a new argument against its existence. In the following decade of meticulous historico-linguistic analysis, historians have increasingly defended the existence of Shungwaya as the origin site of Bantu peoples who eventually migrated south along the coast and west into the mainland, although many scholars disagree about the specific location of the place (Allen 1993; Masao and Mutoro 1988; Nurse and Spear 1985). Regardless of its specific location, its existence in southern Somalia makes a forceful claim for the Bantu origins of the pre-Somali inhabitants of the region, a claim that is increasingly important to the marginalized Somali Bantu inhabitants of and refugees from that region, all of whom have faced generations of discrimination from ethnic Somalis (Eno 1997; Kusow 1995; Luling 2002; Menkhaus 1989).

Shungwaya is one piece of the Somali Bantu history, one that provides a reasonably ancient and proud origin point for the emerging culture group. The other piece is more recent and less illustrious. The Indian Ocean has long been an effective transportation route for people and things. In the nineteenth century, under the Sultanate of Zanzibar, the island became a vibrant hub for the Indian Ocean slave trade. The Zigua, inland people ancestrally located near the island of Zanzibar, were a fruitful community for slavers; their proximity made them a significant source of captive labor to feed the growing trade along the coast. Later in the century, slavers moved more deeply into the continent, building on the already existing practices of human bondage that existed, while the consolidation of transportation made it easier to move people along the coast to serve a growing plantation economy in present-day Somalia, Kenya, Tanzania, and Mozambique. At the peak of the East African slave trade toward

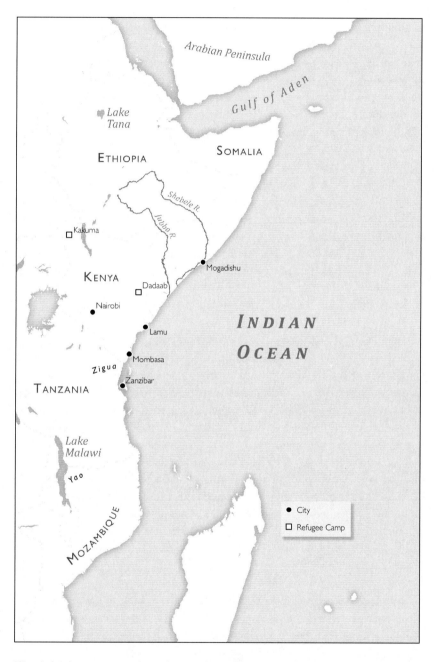

Historical and contemporary places of note for Somali Bantu in East Africa. Map by Dylan Moriarty.

the middle of the nineteenth century, further inland people, including the Yao, the Nyamwezi, and people from near Lake Malawi (also known as Lake Nyasa), became a growing source of labor to feed the slave trade. However, with the arrival of the British fleet and increased oceanic patrols in the 1870s, the slave trade eventually retracted its reach, and slaving picked up again among the Zigua from northern Tanzania (Cooper 1997, 121–22). Consequently, throughout the 1800s a large number of Zigua adults were transported to plantations in southern Somalia; later in the century, a significant population of Yao children were further transported there.

Once in present-day Somalia, these Bantu-speaking groups became central to agricultural production. From the 1830s and 1840s the new arrivals found refuge from slavery in the lower Jubba region, joining the descendants of the original proto-Bantu group. Lee Cassanelli, working from Zigua oral tradition, argues that many Zigua sold themselves into bondage during a severe famine in present-day Tanzania, only to discover upon arrival in the horn of Africa that the enslavement was permanent, a reality that was not common in the system of temporary bondage that they had previously known. Many of these new slaves escaped from the plantations to the interriverine area in the south of Somalia in an effort to walk back to Tanzania (1989, 221). Once in this most fertile part of the country, they established alliances and formed autonomous communities. By the 1860s the flood of slaves into the area increased because of escape, manumission, and British antislavery efforts that disrupted slaving out of Lamu in northern Kenya. At this point, the various groups that would later become known as the Somali Bantu settled into enclaves, sometimes along pre-slavery ethnic lines, sometimes according to plantation location. Founding members became village elders, and the shortage of women resulted in ethnic intermarriage, although Cassanelli notes that there were occasional prohibitions against marriage with women from groups who did not remove the labia minor and clitoris then sew together the labia major—a genital surgery known as infibulation—as part of their rite of passage into adulthood (224–25), an indication of the importance of an initiation ritual for determining cultural identity during a time of crisis, dislocation, and intermarriage, and a practice that will be further discussed in chapter 2.

By the end of the nineteenth century, there were communities of independent farmers living along the Jubba and Shebelle, as well as client farmers who attached themselves to more powerful groups, such as ethnic Somali pastoralists or plantation owners. These agriculturalists developed their own lineage groups and had uncontested rights to the land they cultivated. Cassanelli speculates that these rights were not contested because their herder-patrons were dependent on the agricultural labor, and because many of the farmers were believed to possess supernatural powers, such as control over river animals like crocodiles (1988, 270). In addition, there were still imported slaves performing agricultural work. With the abolition of slavery by the Italians in 1908, many slave holders granted parcels of land to their former slaves, turning them into client farmers. What held these various communities in southern Somalia together was their faith in Islam, the practice of ritual events, and the risks and spoils of war with their neighbors (271–72). However, the cultural situation in the area was diverse, as each generation of slaves formed communities along these rivers, moving from the coastal area further inland, and the cultural character of these communities was affected by preslavery practice and the timing of the trauma of their enslavement. For example, the Zigua communities—in which most slaves had attained adulthood prior to dislocation—retained a considerable amount of their original cultural practices, including language use (Besteman 1999, 64). The Yao—a group in which most of the slaves were dislocated by slavery prior to adulthood—retained fewer of their preslavery cultural practices and became more closely tied to Somali clans, Islam, and the Somali language (67). Each of these groups operated as distinct communities, living and working together, for whom clan affiliation and village identity were most important.

Evolution of Group Identity

Despite the complex and diverse sense of affiliation within these communities, to dominant groups these agriculturalists were identified as part of one large subordinate group. Catherine Besteman notes that, for many former slave societies, group affiliation became distinguishable according to racial characteristics after the adoption of the dominant religion by the subordinate group (1995, 48). In this case, the distinction of slave/infidel evolved into slave/African after many of the Bantu-speaking groups adopted Islam in the late nineteenth and early twentieth centuries. So these complex communities were known to ethnic Somalis as slaves, then former slaves, and later as the ones who have hard hair, a reference to a feature of their African ancestry. This designation distinguished them from the dominant ethnic Somalis, whose self-perception emphasizes their Arabian past and features, or "soft" hair. In fact, these marginalized agriculturalists were subordinated under a number of different regimes during the twentieth century, all of which attributed to them different identities. For the Italians, they were the *liberati*, or those liberated from slavery. For the British, they were the *wagosha*, or people from the forest (50–54). Regardless of name, they were generally subordinates, and their distinguishing features—whether of occupation, physical features, or language usage—marginalized them.

In the early 1970s, anthropologist Virginia Luling wrote an ethnographic study of a single community in southern Somalia that provides a snapshot of community relations in one place in that period of Somali history. She notes that there were great distinctions between pastoralists and agriculturalists, and she describes these distinctions along linguistic and physical lines, noting that the Cushitic speakers have more European features, while the others are more Negroid, with broad noses, full lips, and hard hair; skin colors vary in both groups. At that stage, she noted that there were a number of names for those of more Negroid features, and since all of them were derogatory, she refers to these people as Habash, because it was the term used colloquially. However, she notes that there were further distinctions: Habash claim no slave background and have equal status with ethnic Somali farmers, while the Ooji come from slave origin and belong to the lineage of their former masters. Both groups were also identified as Jerir, which refers to the hard hair, but Luling stuck with the Habash designation through this work (1971, 42–47). Interestingly, group identity changed even within the thirty years between the writing of Luling's dissertation in 1971 and the publishing of it in 2002. In the more recent publication, she notes that Habash, which refers to Abyssinian or Ethiopian origin, can be considered derogatory, so she adopts Jareer, because it is inoffensive. She refuses to adopt the term Somali Bantu, because the group does not speak a Bantu language (2002, 114–15). It is worth noting that, in one of my first encounters with Somali Bantu students in the United States, the teenagers pointed out to me the differences between their hair texture and facial features and those of the ethnic Somalis at the school and named it as a distinguishing difference from ethnic Somalis.

Because her study was not aimed specifically at the Habash/Jerir groups, Luling suggested that those interested in further understanding of such communities should study the material culture and ritual life of these groups, as those pieces seem to connect directly to their preslavery ethnic affiliations in East Africa (47), the key to understanding their identity. This approach was subsequently taken up by Francesca Declich, who argues that, within these local communities, groups engaged in distinctive ritual practices that served to distinguish their identity most clearly and that provided the most authoritative retelling of community history. For example, she argues that the mviko, or matrikin unit, conveyed authority to women, an authority that was lost in the records of colonial administrators, but which continued in women's discourse, ritual song, and personal reminiscence of these groups (Declich 1995a, 94, 102).

Further, Declich argues, performances by mviko groups were indicators of ethnic identity because of their association with initiation rituals, which allowed them to characterize distinctions between groups, particularly as one moved further south into a plurality of dance and ritual practice (1995a, 192).

Working contemporaneously with Declich, the historian Kenneth Menkhaus produced the most detailed tracing of ethnic affiliation within the agriculturalist groups. As a general term, he refers to them as the Gosha (people from the forest) but notes that that they use the word Shambara, which they claim refers to the five ethnic groups within their overarching community. Menkhaus suggests that the word comes from the Shambaa people who were neighbors of the Zigua in nineteenth-century Tanzania because the word is more commonly used in lower Jubba, where there was a greater population of Zigua people. In middle Jubba, the agriculturalists were more likely to have a clan identity within the ethnic Somali social system because they entered into patron-client relationships with them. He further notes that, in lower Jubba in the 1980s, groups were divided along preslavery ethnic origins, including Yao, Nyasa, MoKua, Ngindu, Nyika, and Zigua, but that, after more than a hundred years of existing as communities in Somalia, all but the Zigua had lost command of their ethnic language (Menkhaus 1989, 25–31).

To summarize, before the collapse of the Somali state, the population of non-ethnic Somali agriculturalists living in southern Somalia demonstrated some diversity in their cultural practices, even as they experienced similar historical phenomena, adopted Islam, and used a form of Somali language, at least as a lingua franca. While outsiders identified and marginalized them by their status as former slaves, or through racial features tying them to an African identity, their own identities were determined through initiation rituals and expressive practices tying them to a particular ethnic group, clan affiliation, and/or village identity, a characteristic that had seemingly remained constant since their odyssey in Somalia began in the nineteenth century.

The Collapse of the Somali State

The background changed radically for these communities in the early 1990s, when the state collapsed and the country was engulfed by intra-clan warfare. While the war has been popularly viewed by outsiders as an intra-clan battle over power, the violence and eventual famine visited on southern Somalia had its roots in late twentieth-century land policies. According to Besteman and Cassanelli, this historically marginalized area of Somalia was quietly growing

in importance throughout the 1970s and 1980s. First, the state resettled displaced nomads into the area following the loss of their herds to drought in the
early 1970s, and later transplanted Ogaadeen refugees to the area during the
war with Ethiopia, increasing the number of people needing access to land. In
the meantime, agricultural land became valuable as an investment because
urbanization increased demands on Somalia's natural resources (Besteman
and Cassanelli 2000, 17–19). The state began a land registration program in
1975, which nationalized all land and required farmers to apply for fifty-year
leasehold titles. As a result, farmers who had cultivated the land for generations
lost claim to it, and without title registration for the land, various elites began to
lay claim to it, placing their militias on it while the Barre regime began to seek
control over the resources. Besteman and Cassanelli argue that the civil war
that followed in the 1990s, while it exhibited the elements of clan warfare, was
actually a struggle for wealth and resources (23, 30). Once the war began, the
lower Jubba area was the site of intense battles between the militias, while the
preexisting agriculturalist communities had very little stake in the outcome or
role in the fighting. Menkhaus, who carried out research in southern Somalia
in 1991, describes banditry, assaults by armed gangs, looted food supplies forcing
villagers to resort to using famine foods, the diversion of international food aid
away from the population, and other horrors of war. By mid-1991 children
from the area had malnutrition levels averaging 60 percent, farms were in
ruins, and the farmers were not able to reclaim their rights to the land (Menkaus,
discussed in Besteman and Cassanelli 2000, 150–51). Van Lehman and Eno
note that the southern Somali agriculturalist communities were the backbone
of food production and, as food became scarce in the early 1990s, they became
the targets of banditry, resulting in an escalation of robbery, rape, and murder
(2003, 10). They began to flee in droves to refugee camps along the Somali–
Kenyan border. By 1994 ten thousand Somali Bantu refugees lived in the
Dagahaley, Ifo, Liboi, and Hagadera refugee camps near Dadaab, a semi-arid
town in Kenya's Northeastern Province, where they sought resettlement in
their ancestral home of Tanzania. It is worth noting that several thousand also
fled to refugee camps along the Kenyan coast and in northern Tanzania (10).

Along with the disintegration of the state came the disintegration of cultural
norms protecting vulnerable members of society. In her work, Fowzia Musse
details the diya rules that operated to protect women from sexual violence and,
when it occurred, to determine the appropriate compensation to her because
of the impact that rape, as well as a resulting pregnancy, would have on her
marriageability (Musse 2004, 76–78). However, with the rise of militias, rape
became a common threat. Musse describes the establishment of rape camps by

militias, which kidnapped women from opposing factions or with weak clan affiliations and protections, such as members of these agriculturalist groups. Subgroup affiliation aside, 80 percent of those seeking refuge in Kenya in the early 1990s were women and children (70). However, the flight to refugee camps did not necessarily provide protection. As refugees flooded into them, the growing camps along the border of Somalia and northeastern Kenya were vulnerable to both shifta bandits, who were long established in the area, and Somali fighters. Nowrojee and Thomas detail the vulnerability of relief workers and Kenyan police as well as women and children from the growing refugee population. They also describe how the pattern of violence played out against ethnic and clan affiliation, noting that rapists often asked about clan affiliation to spare their own women from sexual violence. Likewise, victims claimed that political and military developments in Somalia affected patterns of abuse in the camps. In addition, since most of the attackers in the region spoke Somali, there were numerous reports of Kenyan police retaliating against Somali women (Nowrojee and Thomas 1993, 7–8). Musse corroborates the targeting of women from rival clan groups for rape, noting that most of the victims she interviewed indicated that their clan affiliation in southern Somalia played a role, as did looting, robbery, and the targeting of women income earners (2004, 72–73). Ultimately, what is significant is the importance of group affiliation in the collapse of the state's central authority. At this point in the chaos of war and flight from it, ethnic and clan affiliation became paramount for acquiring protection against violence from other members of one's group.

For the diverse non-ethnic Somali groups in southern Somalia, Declich claims that the descent into chaos in the early 1990s destroyed a complex inter-ethnic system of mutual support in southern Somalia, and resulted in large-scale rape of women within the Somali Bantu population in particular. She argues that this phenomenon was a central factor for these groups in fleeing Somalia (Declich 2000, 29, 43–44). As these disparate groups of marginalized agriculturalists with ties to a sub-Saharan past, and with varying degrees of affiliation to the Somali clan structure, arrived in the refugee camps, the aid organizations tasked with administering those camps were instrumental in constructing an overarching Somali Bantu ethnicity in order to categorize them. Van Lehman and Eno explain that, as a result of their arrival date and discrimination against them by other Somali refugees, the Bantus settled along the periphery of the camps, which left them more vulnerable to bandit attacks. As a result, they—like other groups—constructed fortified areas guarded by armed sentries, but they were still disproportionately attacked in comparison to other inhabitants of the camps. Further, the need to collect firewood from the area outside the camp made all refugee women—traditional gatherers of firewood—vulnerable to attack, and the populations on the periphery more vulnerable to retaliation from other groups in the event of sexual violence. As a result, interethnic hostilities often broke out (Van Lehman and Eno 2003, 11–12). It was in this context that these once disparate groups became identified as Somali Bantu. Along with the construction of an overarching identifier, camp administration also deconstructed certain social norms. For example, according to Declich, the camp administration affected the status of Somali Bantu women because they assumed patriarchy within a population that previously placed both genders in a position of some authority. Women, because of their role as diviners and their connection to matrikin ancestors, had social standing before flight into the camps. However, the new ethnic construction happening in the camps excluded women from public space, and this, along with the high prevalence of rape, disempowered Somali Bantu women in particular (Declich 2000, 38–44).

Ultimately, resettlement of Somali Bantu into refugee camps in northern Kenya has proven to be an experience fraught with paradox. The refugee experience has sanctioned an overarching cultural identity out of disparate local communities, while, conversely, it has also radically disrupted the practice of traditional culture by these groups. It was in the camps that these local communities gained recognition as a separate ethnic community by transnational refugee administrative systems, by state actors facilitating their resettlement to the United States, and by other refugee groups. It was here that they became Somali Bantu, a once obscure term for these agriculturalists that had circulated among Italian ethnographers in the 1930s and was discarded, and which was never used locally (Luling 2002, 115). In the camps, for the first time in their history, they petitioned for recognition and gained it, and that status allowed for a separate resettlement program to the United States. But, at the same time, their experience in the camps disrupted local communities and local cultural practices. There was no longer farming to do, so the agriculturalist patterns of life diminished in relevance, particularly for children with no memory of life in Somalia. They also became grouped with agriculturalist counterparts who may speak a different language and have different cultural practices, and with whom they may have had no prior relationship. Finally, the ritual events that distinguished various communities were dislocated, and when practiced, were more public within the vast and crowded camps. In short, the practices that solidified unique cultural identities within Somalia became very difficult for them to conduct, just as they gained status for having a unique cultural identity before the larger world community.

Resettlement in the U.S. Heartland

In recognizing the unique cultural status of the Somali Bantu, the UN High Commission for Refugees came to recognize that this growing population of refugees in the camps would need to be resettled outside of southern Somalia if peace were restored to the nation. As early as 1993, published reports noted that the Bantu minorities from middle Jubba were resisting repatriation to Somalia because of the "persistent and violent discrimination they have faced at the hands of all major Somali factions," and a desire within the population to resettle in their homelands in eastern Africa (African Rights 1993, 48). In the 1990s there were efforts to return them to their ancestral lands in Tanzania and Mozambique, but these were unsuccessful. Consequently, in 2003 the U.S. State Department began to resettle approximately thirteen thousand of them to the United States. This new group of refugees from Somalia was initially directed to fifty-two cities across the United States, selected because they offered a combination of important resettlement resources: ESL programs in the public school systems, access to plentiful jobs at the appropriately unskilled end of the labor market, volunteer agencies experienced in the resettlement of refugees, and enough language resources in the community to assist in adult ESL classes and with the health and welfare needs of the arriving refugees. At a primary resettlement site, the providers of those resources could count on federal and local financial support to assist in the preliminary resettlement. These resources included subsidies for municipal public housing and food vouchers for the new arrivals.

In the decade preceding the arrival of the Somali Bantu, the large Midwestern city that is the focus of this study had become an attractive site for ethnic Somali refugees who composed the first wave of resettlement from the disintegrating East African nation. By 2004, when resettlement of the Somali Bantu began, this city claimed the fourth largest population of ethnic Somali refugees in the United States and, as such, was considered unattractive by resettlement professionals as a resettlement site for an ethnic minority population from the same nation (Walker 2007). At that time, the designated resettlement agency for this population, Jewish Family Services, expected a small population of approximately 160 people and were equipped to assist with their resettlement in the area until June 2005, when the grant would be complete (Zissman 2005).

Within the first year of resettlement, however, the area began to attract a number of Somali Bantu away from their primary resettlement sites in other U.S. states near and far. In the fast-growing network of communication enabled by access to cell phones, word began to spread in the Somali Bantu diaspora

that there were abundant job opportunities there for refugees with little education, and that housing prices were very affordable (Matan 2007). By the summer
of 2005, just when the grant was ending at Jewish Family Services, what had
begun as a trickle of Somali Bantu escalated into a flood. Secondary migrants,
or refugees who moved to the area from their primary sites, numbered around
three hundred, nearly double the population planned for primary resettlement
in the area (Walker 2007). Somali Bantu families were arriving in the city with
no place to live, and they soon so overwhelmed the homeless shelters that those
agencies began to enforce a requirement of residency within the county prior to
receiving homelessness services, and to move the arriving Somali Bantu out of
shelters and onto the streets. In response to the crisis, the refugee resettlement
agency of the mainline Protestant churches, Community Refugee and Immigration Services (CRIS), stepped in to manage the arrival of Somali Bantu refugees
in the city. By the fall of 2007, when I began my research, the number of Somali
Bantu refugees in the area numbered around a thousand (Walker 2007), many
of whom had clustered together at a few large public housing projects around
the southwestern boundary of the city. It was within this emerging Somali
Bantu community where I conducted my field research.

Aims and Methods of the Research

Over the course of their history in the horn of Africa, these various groups of
agriculturalists have been identified in a number of different ways. Typically,
the ones that have been recorded are those attributed to them by outsiders
wielding the power to name them according to whatever features seem most
relevant at any given time. What little we know from within these communities,
however, indicates that cultural identity has been remarkably stable and is
deeply tied to ritual practices generally, and initiation rituals specifically. My
project explores how the disruption of the practice of initiation ritual and integration into the U.S. school system has particularly affected practices of identity
formation, both at the level of group identity and within the life course. This
project did not aim to document how initiation ritual events were practiced in
the past, nor to comprehensively document how they are currently practiced in
diaspora, whether in Kenyan refugee camps or in U.S. resettlement communities. It seemed to me that an effort to document and analyze initiation practices
involving genital cutting was problematic for an initial research study of this
recently arrived group. However, the question of initiation became central to
my research project because, regardless of what is happening in their current

ritual practice, what is clear is that the ritual context has been radically altered by dislocation and resettlement, and much of the identity formation that previously occurred within the ritual context has been disrupted. Nevertheless, young people continue to keep growing into adults, and the community has to find a way to manage this process. The Somali Bantu teenagers in America move between two poles of identity—as something imposed from birth or as a choice among many alternatives (Abrahams 2003, 207–8)—and it seems that both the teenagers and the community are in the midst of identity crisis, one deepened by the disruption of this critical ritual. As a result, these young refugees find themselves in a doubly liminal space. Not only are they betwixt and between childhood and adulthood, but they are also coming of age in a culture group where cultural practice and identity are in flux, gender roles are under considerable pressure, and young people are being integrated into the U.S. system of education, with its American model of adolescence. This study aimed merely to explore what social and cultural tools they grasp to navigate these turbulent waters.

The fieldwork project involved sixteen months of ethnographic research. Initially, I based myself at the McGuffey Welcome Center, one of two sheltered schools for high school age English-language learners in the Municipal Schools at that time. I began my fieldwork at the start of the 2007–8 school year, and continued through the following summer and the first half of the 2008–9 school year, when the students and faculty were moved into a new school building and integrated with the district's other sheltered high school program at Linmoor School. I regularly attended classes at both institutions for a combined total of thirteen months, moving between formal classrooms, informal extracurricular groups, administrative offices, lunchrooms, and the playground. In some instances, I accompanied students and staff on field trips. Aside from some tutoring, I had no institutional role at either welcome center; given my background with African history and cultural practice, however, staff and students came eventually to see me as a resource for understanding the cultural background of the East African students.

In my earliest days at McGuffey, my time was spent observing Citizenship class, as many of the Somali Bantu teenagers were clustered in two sections of this course, and the teachers were eager for insight into these unusual students to help them learn. About two months into my school fieldwork, the school reorganized the students based on language skills, which I describe in chapter 4. From this point, I spent my time in a section each of high, intermediate, and low language learners, following topical courses in Citizenship and Science Learning. During this period of research, I also became a frequent participant in College Club, a lunch program organized by the school nurse to provide health education to students who volunteered for this extracurricular program. As winter turned to spring, and the intramural soccer tournament began, I became an avid follower of Team Africa and also attended most of their matches. Later, as McGuffey integrated with the other district welcome center, the Somali Bantu student population became diluted into a larger number of course sections, which made it less productive to attend classes, as I was unable to speak with the students. This new schedule, however, split the students into two different extended lunch groups, and I found most of my time at the Linmoor Welcome Center was spent in conversation with clusters of Somali Bantu students during those periods, and with available teachers and administrators in the other periods.

As my relationships with students grew, I followed a number of Somali Bantu students into their lives outside school, and I became a regular visitor at Wedgewood Village Apartments, the public housing project that had become home to about a thousand members of the Somali Bantu community. In my earliest days at the complex, I was adopted by a well-connected couple and their extended family, and I often came and went from their apartment. With the arrival of the summer holidays, as my visits became more frequent, it became increasingly difficult to visit any single member of the community routinely, as my arrival typically drew the attention of any number of familiar teenagers, and I became a spontaneous participant in their activities. It was through hanging out with these teenagers that I came to know the wider neighborhood of Wedgewood Village and came to a deeper understanding of their personal histories and plans for the future. During the course of my research, I became involved in the everyday worlds of these Somali Bantu teenagers as they attended school, participated in family life, celebrated ritual events, performed household chores, socialized with one another, played sports, or simply watched television at home. I carried out participant observation research over these sixteen months at school and at home, which were the central locations of their lifeworld at the time.

During this period, I also conducted many informal interviews with the students and their parents. I must highlight, however, that communication was the biggest limiting factor in conducting this study, with noticeable effects on the data that follows. As is noted in chapter 1, members of the group communicate primarily in two different languages, af-Maay and Kizigua. I had no opportunity to learn either of these languages before I began my fieldwork, so with adults, I relied on a combination of Swahili or English that was often interpreted between us by the teenaged members of the community. I had anticipated this difficulty when I selected the focus of my study and chose an age group that had some fluency in English. However, this selection was not without problems of its own. As many a parent and teacher of teenagers will acknowledge, it is not always easy to motivate young people to be self-reflective or even communicative, even when one is operating within the same language. In this case, it was often difficult to obtain direct answers to many of my questions. Consequently, I developed a highly convoluted pattern of communication with the Somali Bantu teenagers, often asking questions about obvious cultural practices in the hope of stimulating explanations and insights. In an effort not to inhibit conversation with them, I took minimal notes during these conversations. I recorded very few interviews, as the use of my digital recorder typically served to silence most teens. Instead, immediately upon leaving the field site, I dictated extensive comments from my notes, observations, conversations, and experiences into my digital recorder as I made the three-hour drive from the research site back to my home.

The study that follows, while offering some insights into identity construction within this refugee community, demonstrates the limits of this methodology. I gained no experience of the verbal arts currently or previously practiced by Somali Bantu, as none were ever shared with me during my field experience. The elder members of the community were unable to communicate them to me, and the teenagers never used any of them in my experience. So this ethnography will have gaps in genres that may be significant to other folklorists. More significantly, my data is driven by observable practice rather than interviews or the collection of verbal texts, an approach that is relatively unusual among folklorists but was necessary in this research context. As a result of the linguistic issues, I am at my most certain about the claims that follow when I describe and analyze what the members of the community do, but I am considerably less certain of the meaning of what was and is said, particularly by those with whom I had the greatest language difficulty. In those wonderful instances when members of the community provided a voice, I have attempted to include it into the study. Despite these limitations on my research, which I hope become increasingly surmountable as my relationship with the community develops in the future, I believe that this project was a valuable place to begin understanding the Somali Bantu and their expressive culture, and I hope it makes a contribution to understanding the experience of teenagers in the midst of cultural and personal dislocation, despite the complications of conducting research in such a limited frame.

Finally, I want to note that Institutional Research Board requirements at the Municipal Schools and my sponsoring institution, the University of

Pennsylvania, recognize the minors who participated in my study as a protected category in human subject research. As such, I was required to obtain consent from them before engaging in research, photographing, videoing, or writing about them, and I am required to conceal their identities by keeping their names confidential. I dutifully obtained consent both from individual teenagers and their legal guardians. Even this seemingly standard practice was complicated by how our individual communities construct adulthood as well as the lack of birth records on these refugees. In many cases, both Somali Bantu teens and adults objected to my practice of concealing individual names (one element of identity), and may authorize me to use their real names as they move into chronological adulthood as recognized in the United States. However, for the purpose of this study, all names of those recorded by official documents as being under age eighteen at the time of my research have been changed. In accord with the wishes of most adults, however, I have used their real names, making changes only in instances that would require me to do so to protect the identity of those minors affiliated with them. In instances where I was uncertain of the chronological age of the individual, I determined their status as adults according to whether they are married, which, as I contend in a later chapter, actually indicates they have achieved the status of adulthood in the Somali Bantu community, regardless of chronological age. Likewise, research protocols that I signed with the school district also require me not to specifically identify the school system by name. In an effort to conform to the spirit, as well as the letter, of this agreement, I likewise have kept the specific location of the district anonymous in this publication. Despite this complication, I hope the following study provides enough ethnographic detail to be meaningful within its U.S. context.

I have begun this work with a brief discussion of the historic and cultural background of a people now identified as Somali Bantu as found in a limited and diverse array of sources, with a particular emphasis on the evolution of this cultural identity and the importance of initiation ritual to forming it among community members. Chapter 1 considers the role of the diasporic Somali Bantu community, located as a village within the U.S. urban landscape, in creating a sense of Somali Bantu identity, with consideration of how that effort is shaped by traditional rites of passage as practiced by the group in Africa. Chapter 2 provides an overview of traditional approaches to becoming an adult. Chapter 3 moves from these traditional practices of passage to an exploration of the role globalized media plays in preparing Somali Bantu boys and girls for culturally appropriate gender roles in the midst of dislocation and re-settlement. Chapter 4 examines modernist approaches to attaining adulthood and considers the concept of identity as it relates to the Somali Bantu at this moment in their history. Chapter 5 moves into the U.S. school system to consider how its practices inadvertently mimic traditional rites of passage and serve to enculturate these young refugee students to modernist values. Chapter 6 explores the emerging nature of wedding rituals and their role in providing these young refugees with a means of completing their passage to adulthood. In the final chapter, I review how the various elements of identity formation are affected as this population moves toward constructing adolescence in the United States.

1

The New Village

The Construction of Somali Bantu Identity
in Everyday Life

*W*edgewood Village Apartments is a cluster of seventy-nine identical, rectangular housing units built of standard orange brick, spread across either side of a half-mile stretch of slightly winding road in the southwestern corner of a large Midwestern city. The apartment complex is bounded to the east, west, and south by a lower-to-middle-income neighborhood of mostly single-family properties. On its north is Sullivant Avenue, a busy, four-lane traffic artery connecting this corner of the city to its urban center. Along Sullivant there are the usual American clusters of gas stations, fast food providers, and commercial shops. A similar neighborhood with identical structures and vendors could be found replicated many times over in America's cities. However, despite its mid-twentieth-century institutional character—and a name that evokes eighteenth-century British china—the unique circumstances of the Somali Bantu community relocated to Wedgewood Village have enabled the compound to become a significant site for developing and practicing Somali Bantu identity. This chapter will explore the aesthetic and social practices that members of the community use to reconstruct the dynamics of southern Somali village life in the space of an urban American housing project. Barbara Kirshenblatt-Gimblett has argued that the indigenous solutions found by city dwellers to express their values and shape the style of their everyday lives is often the only means they have to control those lives (1983). In the case of the Somali Bantu refugees living at Wedgewood Village, these everyday aesthetic and social practices not only express values and provide order to their lives in the midst of widespread disruption but are also the central means by which they inculcate a sense of ethnic identity for their teenagers.

Welcome to the Village

Moving through this area of the city, there is no definitive boundary between traditional working-class America and southern Somali village. Gas stations, dollar stores, and fast food restaurants proliferate as one drives up Sullivant, and the industrial character of the landscape overwhelms the occasional appearance of an East African resident wearing bright, traditional clothes. About a half mile toward the city along Sullivant lies the Westside Mall, a completely nondescript storefront within an aging strip mall, also constructed of generic orange brick, which may have formerly housed a large pharmacy or grocery store. In recent years, however, it has been turned into a Somali shopping center.

Once inside the mall, the external façade of down-at-heel shopping center opens up into an East African bazaar, with vendors clustered in small units throughout the building, their wares spilling out from their cramped quarters into the crowded passageways that wind along, forming concentric circles inside the perimeter of the box-shaped building. Stretched all along a side wall is a

Westside Mall exterior. Photo by author.

Westside Mall interior. Photo by author.

credit union, and along another side wall is a travel agency specializing in flights to East Africa. Along the back, a café sells drinks, samosas, and a variety of East African snacks to an all-male clientele. The clusters of tiny shops scattered elsewhere within the building sell food supplies from Somalia, furniture, fabrics to use for Somali clothing, ready-to-wear fancy dress clothes of both Indian and East African design, and daywear, including used American and Somali clothing. Other shops offer appliance repair, rent African and Indian movies, and offer rentable goods for celebrations. By and large, the proprietors of the individual shops are ethnic Somalis, and the mall is similar to two others that cater to the Somali population clustered in other parts of the greater metropolitan area. Because of its location, the Westside Mall draws many Somali Bantu buyers from the housing estates nearby.

I begin with the shopping mall because it offers a representational pattern of a vibrant aesthetic and social world reminiscent of Somalia enclosed within the aging structures of the post–World War II American landscape found in this part of the city. This pattern is repeated in numerous ways within Wedgewood itself, both inside individual family apartments and in the multigenerational, distinctively clad clusters of Somali Bantu refugees gathered outside in its common spaces. John J. McDermott has pointed out that a neighborhood is not a collection of external structures but is "a complex field of relationships that form an ecological network" (1987, 84–85). The Westside Mall is an important element in the aesthetic ecology of Somali Bantu life in that it supplies consumer goods to the refugee population, goods that provide them some ability to control their surroundings and produce material effects through intentional activity, a central element in the production of locality (Appadurai 1996, 182). Not unlike its role in mainstream American life, the shopping mall enables the continued consumption by Somali Bantu refugees of material culture from East Africa. At the same time, it limits the style and variety of goods available, creating specific trends in aesthetic practices that are then reproduced throughout the housing project, reinforcing a sense of aesthetic continuity within the group, an alternative material universe separate from the surrounding American environment. This sense of continuity aids elders in constructing Somali Bantu identity in the midst of dislocation.

Devoid of its inhabitants, the Wedgewood complex is remarkable only in that it is a sudden, condensed cluster of identical buildings that, despite dominating the immediate surroundings of Wedgewood Drive, virtually disappears as one turns into the adjacent neighborhood. It is, to a large extent, a self-contained island of three-story, uniform housing disconnected from the neighborhood. Each of the buildings in the complex is identical in size and design. There is a single entrance door in the center front of each structure, and a corresponding one at the back. Stairs at each door lead down to a basement level, and upward to two levels above ground. On each hallway there are four doors leading to individual apartments. From the hallway, each apartment building retains the modern industrial character of the built environment. The lighting is low and the carpeting has been darkened by human traffic. Once inside, the front door of each apartment opens into its living room. Upon crossing this threshold, the aesthetic surroundings change drastically from that of a large-scale, aging housing unit, self-described as a village, to a small-scale African dwelling, located within a preexisting kinship and village network. According to the website of the complex, apartment units vary in layout only according to the number of bedrooms in each. Because Somali Bantu families tend to be large, most of them live in three-bedroom units with identical designs. Since the hallway door of every apartment opens into the common space of the living room and dining area, there is easy entry for visitors and a somewhat public space for extended family to gather.

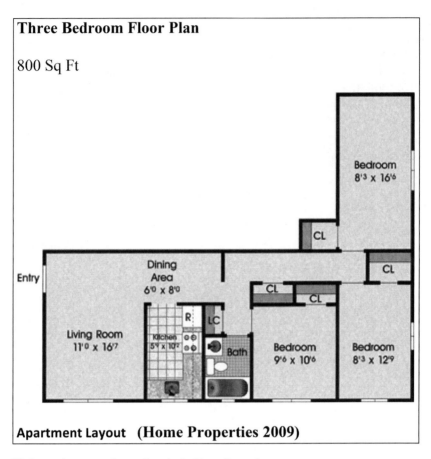

Three Bedroom Floor Plan

800 Sq Ft

Bedroom
8'3 x 16'6

CL

Entry

Dining
Area
6'0 x 8'0

CL

CL

CL

R

LC

Living Room
11'0 x 16'7

Kitchen
5'4 x 10'2

Bath

Bedroom
9'6 x 10'6

Bedroom
8'3 x 12'9

Apartment Layout   (Home Properties 2009)

Wedgewood apartment layout. Drawing by Home Properties.

Despite differences in ethnic backgrounds and pre-resettlement origins, there are a number of aesthetic trends that have emerged throughout the diasporic Somali Bantu community, which allows for some generalization about the décor of individual homes. Most Somali Bantu living rooms are dominated by a divan that stretches along three of the four walls, forming a U-shape, like a sectional sofa, with no permanent back and no legs to lift it off the floor. For back support, most of these divans include a fully detachable, stiff, upright pillow upholstered to correspond with the divan, which is designed with fixed corners to hold the cushions in place where the walls meet. This extensive seating across three walls allows for multiple people to sit comfortably in the living room, while others gather on the linoleum floor or add dining room chairs to the seating arrangements as needed. There is a range of fabric designs available, and while patterns tend to be vibrant, the colors are often muted in comparison to the decorations in the rest of the room. Often, large decorative cloths, also worn by women to carry children or protect clothing, are draped at various places on the divan, usually to provide a space for a smaller child to sleep on the cushions, or to protect the upholstery from spills or other kinds of accidents.

In addition to these cloths, many Somali Bantu families cover the walls of the living room from ceiling to floor in larger, vibrant cloths with distinctive patterns. With few exceptions, the elaborate fabric is attached high on each wall and falls to the floor, giving the appearance that the cloth acts as the wall itself. These decorative cloths typically are spread across the perimeter of the common space, sometimes covering windows. The cloths can be made of lightweight, breezy material, although in some households the draperies are made of heavy fabric and act more like tapestries. Since the arrival of the Somali Bantu, these ersatz draperies have been the cause of some controversy in a number of communities. The refugees have faced resistance to their use from landlords and health officials, who cite myriad concerns about them, including their propensity to provide shelter for bugs and, when they cover doorways and windows, their potential as a fire hazard. Despite this, the cloths remain a popular decorating tool within Somali Bantu homes. At Wedgewood, the cloths rarely cover hallways or doors, a compromise with local building managers that has enabled the cloths to remain in place on walls. In a very material way, the hangings demonstrate the level of affluence in each household, with the most elaborate wall coverings typically evident in the homes of large families with older, income-earning children and greater authority within the community. In those homes with fewer resources, walls remain partially or wholly uncovered.

The wall hangings are a uniquely Somali Bantu trend in home décor. In my initial research with this community, this full enclosure of rooms seemed to offer a way to separate age and gender groups within a household. However, as my fieldwork continued, this use has diminished, and the cloths seem to play less of a functional role and more of an aesthetic one. The hangings are a point of great pride, and my questions about them were typically answered by the matriarch, who routinely indicated that these coverings were the natural way to maintain a domestic space. I could get very little response by way of further explanation, although in the apartment of one family that had removed the cloths to comply with building standards, the mother also admitted that she found the bare white apartment walls to be simply ugly. Even without covering doors and windows, they are a strikingly effective way to cut off the outside world from the inside one, a means of enclosing the home, a tactic of consumption

Basra Hassan Mataan with a grandchild inside her home. Photo by author.

Ceiling covering in a Somali Bantu home, ca. 2008. Photo by author.

in which the Somali Bantu consumer manipulates the institutional housing project to create a habitable space (Certeau 1984, xix–xxi). To enter into the most heavily decorated of these apartments is to enter a wholly African space, to leave behind the sensual experience of America, sometimes even its sunlight, airflow, and sounds, and to enter a less rigidly built, more flowing space, one that contains vibrant color. The most significant aspect of the cloths is that they provide a zone of aesthetic comfort, an enclosure that removes the Somali Bantu home from the U.S. environment that surrounds it.

In addition to these wall coverings, the more elaborately decorated apartments also contain ceiling coverings. While some ceiling coverings are made of the same cloths and tapestries as are common on walls, there is a growing trend toward using a covering particular to ceilings: a large white cloth from which dangles vibrantly colored patterns of crocheted yarns that form concentric boxes. When suspended, these crocheted designs hang down over the living rooms near lighting fixtures. Unlike the drapery hangings, the ceiling coverings are not typically found in local Somali shops but are hand made by female members of the community who create them at home and sell them for approximately

forty dollars a covering. Like the wall coverings, the ceiling coverings contribute
to a sense of enclosure within the living room in which none of the surrounding
infrastructure is exposed.

Despite its sense of enclosure and resistance to the surrounding U.S. culture,
most living rooms contain a ubiquitous American item: the television, which is
often ensconced in an elaborate entertainment center, sometimes with one or
two other sets. In many homes, the television is routinely left on, transmitting a
steady stream of U.S. culture into the carefully constructed enclosure. Patterns
of television use will be discussed in chapter 3, but it is worth noting here that its
offerings contribute to the dynamic swirl of activity within the space. For beyond
the aesthetic zone of comfort it provides, the living room in each apartment is
the site of most domestic activity. Multiple family members gather there to visit,
and meals are shared there. Higher-status members, generally men, elders, and
guests, sit on the divan and eat from individual plates off a small table brought
to them, while lower-status members of the community, generally adult females
and children, eat from a seated position on the floor off a common plate. At all
times of day, it is common to find children and babies napping on the divan
and toddlers groomed, changed, and entertained all in this space. Ultimately,
the living room is a space dominated by women, who use it for shared household and caregiving labor, entertainment, and dance, particularly when celebrating community events in the absence of men. Teenage boys and men move
in and out of the space temporarily, typically for a specific need. Women and
children cluster in it.

Beyond the living room lie the kitchen and what the apartment management designates as the dining area. Since most families eat in the living room,
the dining space serves typically as an extension of the living room. For those
families who have a computer, the space will often include a work station for it.
Generally, the dining area serves as a transitional space into the more private
areas of the home, since proceeding from it there is a hallway to the bathroom
and bedrooms of the unit. While cloths are not generally hung to obstruct the
hallway at Wedgewood, many Somali Bantu families hang some kind of visible
obstruction, such as beads, at the entrance to the hallway to separate it from
the common space at the front of the apartment. With the exception of teenage
boys visiting each other, it is unusual for guests of any type to enter freely in and
out of that part of the apartment as they do in the living rooms of each home.
Bedrooms in individual apartments are typically shared according to gender,
with the senior couple, in those households that have one, sharing the remaining
bedroom. The kitchen lies in the public area off the dining room and adjacent
to the living room. It is a galley kitchen, built for the comfort of a single cook,

while Somali Bantu food preparation often occurs collectively in the living room. Vegetables are cut, eggs are cracked, and mixers run in the midst of toddlers, gossip, rerun action movies, and videotaped weddings of other Somali Bantu refugees. At Wedgewood, the living rooms of homes offer a sensory assemblage, in which "out of bits and pieces, some old, some new, some thrown away, some kept out of nostalgia, [the Somali Bantu] assemble a new environment and return life and meaning to these fragments" (McDermott 1987, 95). Aesthetically, the elements of the mass-produced apartment space, identical to that of its neighbors, are combined with the colors and designs of African textiles, creating a sense of self-contained enclosure, through which the sights and sounds of American entertainment intrude in competition with the daily noises of multiple children and the practice of female domestic chores.

Ethnic Dynamics and Maintenance of Boundaries

At Wedgewood, the art of assemblage is most concentrated in the home, but it is an aesthetic that echoes throughout other elements of the landscape and, in many ways, represents the construction of Somali Bantu identity, itself an assemblage of ethnic identities and preflight relationship patterns. In addition to its use in the home, the next most distinctive display of assemblage is in the pattern of dress worn by the teenage girls. In what has come to be almost a uniform, the girls incorporate American, African, and Islamic elements into a pastiche of items and textures distinctive to both their age group and ethnicity. Just as the more senior women have used the living rooms of their homes as a canvas on which they express cultural identity, the teenage girls display their group affiliation with clothing. The more traditional pieces of the ensemble are a long, full skirt that drapes to the floor and often displays a decorative partial underskirt or hem, and an elaborate combination of head coverings and colorful scarves draped over their heads and shoulders. Completing this ensemble are American elements, including layered T-shirts, sweatshirts, sweaters, and blouses, as well as highly decorative, backless sandals that are worn year-round outside the home and replaced with more pragmatic footwear only while commuting to and from school during the winter. Under the long skirt, Somali Bantu teenage girls often wear a pair of standard American blue jeans.

The American elements of this uniform are an improvisation by the teenagers here, probably brought on initially by their easy access to used clothing, and which now serve to distinguish young women from their female elders, who tend to wear large, shapeless dresses that cover the whole body, rather

Maryan dressed for school. Photo by author.

than an assemblage of American and East African clothing. These teenage improvisational elements, as well as the vibrant colors and textures of the fabrics they use, have become a way for individual girls to demonstrate creativity and a sense of style while conforming to the codes of modesty expected within a Muslim community. Hansen has noted that the use of second-hand clothing in Zambia allows individuals to improvise with Western clothing that is not an imitation of the West, but a form of "improvisation in which the meaning and value of this clothing is constructed anew on local terms" (Hansen 2010, 51). This observation is true of the Somali Bantu girls. In addition, the aesthetic style of the teenage girls has also become the way social service providers and school officials—whose records categorize Somali Bantu students interchange-ably as "Somali," "African," or "Black"—to distinguish them from their ethnic Somali counterparts, who tend to dress conservatively in monochromatic colors and incorporate no visible American elements into their dress. The Somali Bantu girls have become the identifiable representative of the overarching ethnic group because the assemblage of color, texture, and multicultural influence serve as a marker of Somali Bantuness to outsiders.

In her historical research on the nineteenth-century Indian Ocean slave trade, Laura Fair notes a correlation between ethnic identity claims and dress among Yao and Nyasa, forbears to the Somali Bantu displaced along the coast by slavery. She argues that as members of these groups moved away from these preslavery ethnic identity claims, they increasingly adopted the dress of free persons or created new forms that hid ethnic distinctions (Fair 1998, 65–67). The distinctively teenage mixing of American and Islamic dress patterns appears to be the first step in a similar process among these transplanted adolescents. At the moment, the teenage girls seem to have taken an assemblage approach to dressing that incorporates both American and Somali Bantu elements, but there was some indication during my field research that the girls want increas-ingly to blend in sartorially with the mainstream U.S. culture and thereby dis-card ethnic affiliation, at least for brief periods. Soon after I learned of her impending marriage, for example, sixteen-year-old Timiro shyly revealed to me a photo of herself stored on her cell phone, a device that is typically gifted to a young woman by her fiancé following a formal engagement. In the photo, which was taken of her upper body in what appeared to be a bedroom, Timiro appeared as a young American. Her hair was uncovered and combed back in a Western style, and she wore a blazer and considerable makeup. Although the clothing was quite conservative by American standards, the photo shocked me, and my surprise caused Timiro to giggle in response. She would offer no details about the production or circulation of the photo, just a smile of pride that she might be able to pass herself off as a young American woman. I learned little about this activity from the other Somali Bantu girls, but other teachers at the school described similar displays on the cell phones of other Somali Bantu girls rumored to be engaged. Pravina Shukla notes that the act of dressing oneself is a way of asserting power and identity within the dynamics of everyday life and the limits of surrounding expressive culture, particularly for women living within a culture dominated by men (2008, 13). Among the Somali Bantu this very private effort to experiment with American identity through self-presentation seems to be limited to girls who have already contracted marriage, an impending identity shift within the life course that seems to mark the attainment of adulthood among the teenage girls. It may also indicate that the surrounding expressive culture is increasingly less limited as women move forward in the life cycle.

Ethnic Identity at Large

For the moment, however, the vibrantly dressed women have made the Somali Bantu community at Wedgewood a dominant feature of the landscape. Women of all ages cluster outdoors in good weather with large families of children and elders, and move past other groups to interact with other Somali Bantu. Their limited interaction with blacks, whites, Asians, and ethnic Somalis is a marked contrast with the way community members interact with one another. While each individual apartment makes up a specific defined family space, in reality, members of the community move freely throughout one another's homes with little effort made to prevent access, particularly among women. In those instances when doors off the common hallways are locked, they are routinely thrown open for other Somali Bantu refugees without any effort at preliminary identification. As is common in African village life, women share resources and services, such as food and babysitting, with extended kin and neighbors. This sense of community identity has been strengthened by the way resettlement occurred in this city: many of the housing project inhabitants are related by prior family or village ties in Somalia. Despite the fact that they often identify as members of differing ethnic groups, their way of living in the project demonstrates yet another pattern of assemblage that defines the community. The ecological network to which McDermott referred has been, despite the violence of repeated uprooting and repotting, transplanted wholly from Somalia. If, as he notes, the strength of the network lies beneath the surface, than this preexisting network of relationships has served as a root system, anchoring the larger sense of group affiliation to the new, urban landscape (McDermott 1987, 84–85).

Members of the Somali Bantu community in the area describe themselves as belonging almost exclusively to two main ethnic groups: Mushunguli (also known as Wazigua) and Maay-Maay (generally made up of Yao), whose histories were discussed in greater detail in the introduction. In resettlement, the claim of ethnic identity is paradoxical. On the one hand, members of each group are rigid in their sense of ethnic identity because it is determined by kinship and is further reinforced by domestic language use. As noted in the introduction, the language and culture differences among the various groups can be quite extensive. In practice, the Somali Bantu who identify as Mushunguli speak Kizigua at home, and are able to move easily into other Bantu languages, such as Swahili. Because their language communities were more isolated and they had to navigate the Somali state, they generally are also fluent in af-Maay, a Cushitic language sometimes described as the southern Somali dialect of standard Somali (af-Maxaa). By contrast, most non-Zigua do not understand or speak any Bantu languages and are limited in their language use to af-Maay, English, and any Swahili they picked up while in Kenyan refugee camps. Beyond language, members of the community also note physical distinctions between the two groups in addition to the ones they use to differentiate Somali Bantu from ethnic Somalis. Mushunguli tend to have rounder faces and bodies, for example, than their Maay-Maay counterparts, and are often shorter and darker in skin color. On the other hand, beneath the seeming naturalness of ethnic identity, the common history of Somali place, long-term dislocation, and eventual resettlement has rendered many aspects of the ethnic distinction meaningless in the everyday practices of teenage members of the community.

Despite the differences of language use and physical appearance that make up ethnicity, the more significant dynamic at Wedgewood is the presence of extensive kinship networks within the compound. Within the chaos of flight and resettlement, the Somali Bantu community at Wedgewood has a complex and intact web of family and village relations, which has supported the effort to reproduce traditional life. In order to provide a specific example, I will trace the kinship network of a highly influential Mushunguli couple within the estate, Mohamed Abuukar Mansuur and Basra Hassan Mataan. It should be noted that what follows is not meant to be a complete tracing of all kinship relations within the estate, as it is often difficult to obtain details on marriages and deaths that occurred prior to resettlement, and thus whether remarriages are the result of a death or a formal divorce, or are in fact a polygamous relationship. Subsequently, it is also difficult to confirm whether those acting as parents are stepparents, adoptive parents, aunts, uncles, or actual birth parents. However, this very limited sketching should illustrate the complexity of kinship relations at this one housing project.

Abuukar and Basra were married around 1990 as the Somali state neared collapse. For both adults, this was not a first marriage. Basra and her first husband, who died in Somalia, had seven children together. All five of her surviving children from that marriage had moved into units at Wedgewood within the two years preceding my fieldwork, and those households include three co-located spouses and a total of fifteen grandchildren as of May 2008. The status of Abuukar's first family is less clear, as is the whereabouts of his first wife, although it seems that at least some of his children from the first marriage live in the Wedgewood complex. Since their marriage, Abuukar and Basra have had two children together, who were teenagers at the time of this fieldwork and lived with them in their shared apartment, as did the teenage son of one of Basra's daughters who died in Africa along with her husband and four of their children. Because many of the family members share apartments, Basra's immediate family collectively claims four apartment units scattered across the housing complex.

In addition to her immediate family, Basra has members of her birth family living in the estate. Her sister Malyuun Mataan lives in Wedgewood along with her nine children from two marriages. In addition, the widow of Basra's brother also lives at Wedgewood with at least three of their children and a healthy collection of grandchildren. Likewise, Abuukar has extended birth family living at Wedgewood. His cousin, Ibrahiin Hanad, lives nearby, and shares an apartment with his second wife and their children while his teenage son from the first marriage, Haaruun, lives in a second apartment with another Somali Bantu teenager. Haaruun is related through his mother to Ibraahin, a teenager who lives with his widowed mother and blind sister at Wedgewood. Furthermore, Ibraahin is also a cousin to Mako, who lives in the estate with her mother and a mix of children from her mother's four marriages. Mako's situation is a rare one at the estate in that it crosses lines of ethnicity. Although her father was Mushunguli, Mako and her mother's family claim ethnicity as Maay-Maay, and Mako insists she only speaks one African language, af-Maay, although she often appears to understand Kizigua to some extent. With this exception of Mako, all of the families so far identified are Mushunguli. This very limited tracing of family relationships accounts for eleven separate apartment units at the housing estate.

The extensive kinship network is not unique to the Mushunguli families, although it is somewhat less prominently displayed among those identifying as Maay-Maay. For example, Kaariye Iman and his wife Haajiro also live at

Wedgewood in a block that neighbors that of Basra and Abuukar. Haajiro has been designated as Kaariye's official spouse from among his cowives, a selection that is required of polygamous refugees for resettlement in the United States in order to conform to U.S. marriage laws. His other wife, Maryan, reportedly remains at the Kakuma refugee camp in northern Kenya with five of their children. One of Maryan and Kaariye's children, Beydan, has been diagnosed with a learning impairment, so she came to the United States as part of the official family, along with four children from Kaariye and Haajiro's marriage, which has subsequently produced another child, nicknamed Obama by his foreign-born brothers and sisters. The whereabouts of Haajiro and Kaariye's three older, married children is currently unclear. Kaariye and Haajiro's children, among whom I am most familiar with Heybe and Haajiro, are first cousins to another teenager I came to know well, Tahlil, who lives across the street at Wedgewood in the household of an uncle, his wife, and a six-person mix of his young cousins and siblings taken in after the death of both his parents. Interestingly, although I had worked with Tahlil, Haajiro, and Heybe for months at their school, none of these teenagers acknowledged the family relationship to me until late in my fieldwork. In general, the Maay-Maay students I encountered were typically less eager to trace out patterns of kinship than their Mushunguli counterparts.

Return to the Village

In addition to their kinship network, it is important to note that both groups are part of an intertwined pre-refugee village network. Regardless of ethnic affiliation, most of these families have long-standing ties to one another that cross ethnic lines and have provided important stability to the teenagers throughout the turbulence of their lives. Maryan, for example, the only daughter of Basra's second marriage, shares a personal history with Maay-Maay girls Timiro and Dahabo stretching back to their early childhoods in the same village. The three teenagers have remained co-located through two teeming refugee camps and resettlement through at least two American cities. However, sixteen-year-old Timiro's recent marriage and seventeen-year-old Dahabo's impending one portend relocation for both brides, moves that have been particularly destabilizing for Timiro and Maryan. In a similar vein, Ibraahin and his cousin Haaruun, both Mushunguli, have a long-standing on-again, off-again friendship with Kaariye and Haajiro's son, Heybe, a Maay-Maay. The three, who have reputedly been instrumental in organizing Somali Bantu gang activity at

Wedgewood, have developed a pattern of fighting one another and offering one another refuge from parents and other authority figures both in the American urban landscape and in the camps. Likewise, Tahlil, the Maay-Maay teenager adopted by his uncle and a cousin to Heybe, was so ubiquitous at the home of Mahdi, the orphaned Mushunguli grandson of Basra, that when I began to map out Mahdi's extended family during one of my visits there, and I playfully asked Tahlil where I should fit him in, his response, "I don't know, Miss, I just live here," elicited laughs of recognition from the assembled Mushunguli family.

In a postconflict attempt to define the Somali Bantu, Catherine Besteman has argued that they are "a group of people of very different origins living and working together in a geographical area" (1995, 53). If a network of relationships transplanted from the African village onto the American one has defined the group, its transplantation has helped preserve a pattern of social interaction in the midst of a somewhat hostile urban environment. The free movement between homes and the sharing of resources noted earlier seems largely unaffected by the seemingly rigid barrier imposed by preexisting ethnic identity. Hermann Bausinger pointed out that what truly provides unity within a village is not shared identity nor cooperation among its inhabitants—something that rarely exists in the European villages that were his concern despite the many idealizations that assumed otherwise—but rather a "unity of place," a notion from drama theory that notes that the actors simply share the place in which action occurs, action that includes a variety of characters, conflicts, tensions, and motives, and which leads to interrelated events affecting the whole community (1990, 34). In their move to Wedgewood, many of the Somali Bantu refugees have managed to retain the unity of place they shared prior to flight from Somalia by preserving the network of family and village connections from their original village. By settling together into a vast but closely linked set of uniform housing units, the community has preserved these relationships and thereby transferred the unity of place they knew in the African village. In turn, it has enabled an overarching sense of shared identity among the teenagers.

Essentially, the Somali Bantu refugees at Wedgewood have successfully adapted the postindustrial housing project into an African village. What has emerged at Wedgewood is an overarching Somali Bantu practice of shared cultural identity, one that allows for the ongoing significance of ethnicity and language within it, but which also places great importance on the experience of common locality prior to flight from Somalia and within the Kakuma and Daadaab refugee camps. In his seminal work on the cultural construction of a sense of place, Keith Basso argued that this sense of place is not merely individual, but eventually "gives way to thoughts of membership in social groups, of participation in activities that transcend the concerns of particular people, of close involvements with whole communities and their enduring historical traditions" (1996, 85). While his argument draws from his work in a rural Apache community long entrenched within their particular landscape, the sense of place remains important even within a group of displaced refugees settling into an urban area. Forced from their previous settlement, the social group has invested its wisdom and its knowledge of historical traditions into an extensive network of relationships with people who also shared that place and then have transplanted these relationships into the new place, thereby constructing locality within the urban housing estate.

Locality Production and the Other

This project of constructing locality, notes Arjun Appadurai, often involves deep attachments to immediate surroundings—in this case, within the co-located network—which are more important than cooperation with the nation-state. His assessment that this happens because people in a group eventually need to differentiate themselves from those in other groups in their neighborhood (1996, 191) is particularly true of Somali Bantu interactions with other ethnic groups within the estate. Wedgewood Village has a diverse population, and its seventy-nine buildings house African Americans, European Americans, ethnic Somalis, and a small, recently arrived settlement of Chinese refugees. Because space within the housing complex is allocated based on family size and unit availability, all of these diverse groups share buildings at Wedgewood but interactions between ethnic groups are fairly limited. In fact, ethnic Somalis have increasingly disappeared from view, although they remain inhabitants of the housing project. Whites and Asians have very little interaction with members of the Somali Bantu community, moving in different circles throughout the complex. The most noteworthy relationship that has developed between the Somali Bantu community and outsiders is with the African American community, and it is a relationship that is fraught with tension. Almost universally, Somali Bantu refugees express fear of what they describe as "The Blacks," a designation that refers specifically to African Americans rather than to any native-born African group, and this preoccupation with potential violence affects how teenage members organize routine activities within the estate.

For teenage girls, their already limited independence is further curtailed by safety concerns. Unless they are accompanied by extended family, young women tend to congregate indoors, so their contact with African Americans is limited to quick exchanges in common areas of buildings. One day, for example, while Maryan was taking me to visit Timiro, we encountered an African American woman at the back stoop of the building talking with her teenage son. Rather than pass around the pair to gain access to the door, Maryan politely stopped and excused herself, wishing both of the occupants a good day before proceeding into the building. The greeting was remarkable in two ways: first, because Maryan executed such a precisely American ritual of formal greeting in the first place, and because she used very formal and articulate English to do so. Until this exchange, I had never seen Maryan greet anyone older than her without waiting for his or her acknowledgment first and then responding exuberantly with smiles and an outstretched hand. Furthermore, her use of English in this instance seemed rehearsed, more reminiscent of formal exchanges memorized from tapes in foreign-language classes than Maryan's ordinarily playful speech patterns. Once we were inside the building, Maryan confided to me that Timiro lives in a dangerous building because it has a lot of blacks living in it, and as a result, Timiro's father has restricted her movements outside the apartment. Later in the day, as we made our way back through the estate, Maryan studiously avoided the building, circling around it rather than taking the most direct route through it.

This concern with violence by blacks, while obvious in the behavior of teenage girls, is almost obsessive among teenage Somali Bantu boys, who more frequently wander in and out of homes and engage in group activities outdoors. Most of them report a state of constant tension and conflict with their African American counterparts. In an early conversation, a group of five teenage Somali Bantu boys explained to me that, if they were caught alone by African American gang members, they would be beaten. Later that summer, Tahlil explained that there was a lot of fear and hiding inside the housing estate because fighting between the two groups of youths had escalated. According to Tahlil, some of the African American youths, who claim to be fourteen or fifteen but are actually older, seek out younger African kids and pick on them to start fights. As a result, many of the Somali Bantu teens have begun to form their own gangs and retaliate against the blacks. A similar conflict had happened the previous summer, and Tahlil had come to know some of the older teenagers and young adults in the black community at Wedgewood as they attempted to sort it out. As a result, Tahlil reflected no fear of the African American community. In fact, as we spoke, two large African American men in their twenties approached us and exchanged friendly greetings with him, and Tahlil seemed to roam freely around the estate with few safety concerns.

Despite this instance of rapprochement, narratives and fear of escalating violence abound, particularly among teenage boys. Other teenage boys describe being in constant fear of black aggression whether commuting to and from school, within the estate, or moving around the city. In actual fact, among social service providers and teachers, Wedgewood estate is considered to be relatively safe as housing projects go, particularly in daylight, and it raises the possibility that African Americans may have become a source of anxiety that has been displaced from the Somali Bantu experience of being a minority population with little power in Somalia, and from their experience as refugees. In that early group conversation with Somali Bantu boys, the teenagers put the subject of African American gang violence into a larger picture of displacement and fear, describing a constant threat from Maasai guards at the Kakuma and Dadaab refugee camps to set dogs on them, and from Sudanese refugees who were regarded as particularly violent and hateful in the massive camps. Into the midst of this multivocal description of the difficulties of the camps, seventeen-year-old Heybe interjected that he longs to return to Nairobi, Kenya, "because it has no gangsters." The boys in the group happily joined this turn in conversation, boasting about this African city with "buildings raised to the sky," but where they would be free from violence directed at outsiders. In fact, when I objected to the characterization of Nairobi as being crime free, Heybe persisted: "Even thieves there do not want to hurt you, just take your money and go away; they use knives there, but here there are guns." In fact, most of the teenage refugees have a very limited experience of Nairobi, having passed through it briefly en route to the United States after years in the camps in remote northern Kenya. However, this short passage may have been the only period of their lives where they felt protected from violent interethnic rivalries in which they had little access to weapons or power, which explains their perception of Nairobi as a haven, instead of the crime-plagued city perceived by many of its other inhabitants and visitors.

Back at Wedgewood, there were few commonly agreed-upon instances of actual gang violence against the Somali Bantu—a nighttime shot through Haaruun's apartment window seems to be the exception—but the perception of threat from gangs of "Blacks" remained constant, particularly for teenage boys. In fact, despite this overriding anxiety, what has developed among the boys is a paradoxical relationship with the culture of black America. Despite their fear of African Americans, the teenage refugee boys are far more likely than other members of the community to emulate the hip-hop culture that surrounds them. This paradox was most striking during the school outing to a skating rink

Somali Bantu teenager dressed for school. Photo by author.

described briefly in the introduction. Throughout the day, many of the Somali Bantu boys displayed an intimate knowledge of hip-hop music, lyrics, and dancing, and this knowledge seemed to be in direct proportion to each individual's reputation as part of a burgeoning Somali Bantu gang engaged in thieving and reprisals against blacks at Wedgewood. Furthermore, this pattern is highly noticeable in the way the teenage boys dress. With few exceptions, the teenage boys wear low-hanging, baggy trousers and T-shirts or sweatshirts emblazoned with images of African American athletes or entertainment figures. Caps, shoes, and other accessories from U.S. sports are often prized and worn regardless of their appropriateness to the weather. In some respects, the adoption of hip-hop dress camouflages the refugee teen boys, often making it difficult for those without a preexisting relationship to them to differentiate them from their African American peers.

Space, Ritual, and Practice

This ability to blend in is a striking point of distinction from the practice of female members of the community who, as noted earlier, provide the visible face of Somali Bantuness to outsiders by how they dress. Their movement distinguishes them as well, as the teenage boys move throughout the public areas of the housing estate independently, while the teenage girls limit their interactions to the living rooms of other Somali Bantu households and move in groups around the estate. In addition, the multiple layers of covering that the girls routinely wear not only preserves a sense of modesty appropriate to Muslim practice in East Africa but also marks them as separate from the surrounding cultures, and therefore inaccessible to members of the surrounding groups. These gendered social practices are often tied in ethnographic literature to ritual practices that construct gender in the first place. In her ethnographic work in Sudan, for example, Janice Boddy noted that initiation practices involving genital cutting within the Hofriyati community she studied serve to enclose female genitalia while exposing those of the males, making gender a cultural construct instead of simply a biological one, and creating a complementarity between genders that extends out in other adult social practices (1989, 56). Just as the enclosure of the womb created by infibulation renders the womb like an oasis, women's spaces throughout that community are characterized by enclosure. Houses, for example, often enclose the women's areas, which serves to protect the young while men move more freely outside the home (73–74). This connection between ritualized initiation practices and the gendered organization of community space has also been observed in other African communities. T. O. Beidelman notes that the rites of passage among the Kaguru also construct gendered individuals who operate in distinctive spheres. For example, Kaguru males, once circumcised, move from their mother's home because the hearth is linked metaphorically with the vagina, and its control is limited to adult women. Following initiation, Kaguru women have influence over the private and men over the public, as space and sexuality are inextricably linked through initiation ritual (Beidelman 1991, 448).

In my earlier description of the aesthetics of Somali Bantu apartments at Wedgewood, I noted that the living rooms are distinctly female spaces where most of the domestic labor is carried out, and that they serve to provide a sense of enclosure from the surrounding U.S. culture. Likewise, the pattern of gendered social practices within the larger housing estate mirrors the distinction between public and private spheres noted among the Hofriyati and Kaguru and suggests that, among the Somali Bantu, there is a similar connection between initiation practices and the organization of space that they have implemented in resettlement. The living rooms, although easily accessible to other members of the Somali Bantu community, and female members in particular, provide a womblike enclosure where children are nurtured while women and girls are protected from the surrounding environment.

In contrast, the male efforts to reproduce culture have focused on creating a distinctly Somali Bantu public space. In my initial research efforts within the community, my access was often brokered by a series of middle-aged men, each of whom was attempting to establish himself as a leader within the community. Each seemed to have a different constituency within the growing Somali Bantu population, a different history in southern Somalia and resettlement, and an incomprehensibly complex relationship with the leadership of the better-established ethnic Somali community organizations in the city. Despite their many differences, each articulated the same solution to the vast problems facing the Somali Bantu community: the creation of a community center. Each one explained to me that a community center would allow them to conduct English as a Second Language classes for adults and young people struggling in schools, offer job training and parenting classes, provide cultural education to their children, and offer a site for community celebrations. In contrast to the women's spaces, where Somali Bantu culture was quietly but steadily being reproduced, the men's clamor for a public space was loud and constant, but largely unproductive. However, they continued to argue that, without a public space, the Somali Bantu of the area would not have a community. In March 2008 one of the faction leaders succeeded in creating such a center near Wedgewood, and he seems to have used it intermittently for some educational programs. It is interesting to note that my knowledge of this center came not through members of the Somali Bantu community at Wedgewood but from an American teacher hired to help with the classes. None of the families I had come to know there used the center for community celebrations. Religious and family events continue to be celebrated in the home or within the confines of the housing estates, while the community center offers a public face for the evolving ethnic group to multiple constituencies in the greater metropolitan area.

Conclusion

Within the refugee community at Wedgewood, there are a number of practices that express values and shape the style of their everyday lives, and these practices are some of the most effective ways that senior community members use to reproduce a distinctive Somali Bantu ethnic identity for their teenage members. In effect, members of the Somali Bantu community have reconstructed an alternative East African universe within the landscape of the postindustrial apartment complex, a universe that reinforces an emerging cultural identity through domestic aesthetic practices, the co-locating of prediasporic kinship and village networks, and a complex maintenance of division between themselves and other marginalized ethnic and racial groups within the project. In her work on the American county fair, Leslie Prosterman points out that the aesthetic criteria that operates at a Midwestern county fair also orders everyday aesthetic life and social relations within the community (1995, 166). At Wedgewood, the aesthetic criteria practiced by the Somali Bantu reinforce an identity based on two differing ideals. On the one hand, there is a clear reinforcement of assemblage in decoration practices and ethnicity within the emerging community. On the other hand, social relations are ordered to maintain divisions both between genders and between themselves and outsiders. It is in this expression of these values through the shaping of everyday life where teenage members of the community learn a sense of Somali Bantu identity.

2

Attaining Adulthood 1

Rites of Passage in Traditional African Contexts

*I*n the previous chapters, I have pointed out the importance of initiation ritual in constructing identity within the Somali Bantu community historically, as well as how it affects the current social practices of village life as reconstructed in a U.S. urban housing project. The aim of this chapter is to provide background on a central model for attaining adulthood available to the Somali Bantu community who participated in this study: their rites of passage. The Somali Bantu, like many other East African culture groups, traditionally celebrate the passage from childhood to adulthood with a culturally specific ritual of initiation characterized by a short but intense period of transition between these two stages of the life course, rather than the open-ended period of adolescence and formal education they have encountered in joining the U.S. school system. If these teenagers had not fled from southern Somalia as children, they would have been initiated within their local communities in much the same way as their parents were: as members of gendered peer groups, they would have undergone ritually performed and communally celebrated cutting of their genitalia and, in the isolated healing period immediately following, they would have been instructed by community elders on their new roles as adult men and women members of the group before rejoining the community. In this model, three different elements of identity—gender, culture group, and status within the life course—are entangled in a ritual that includes both embodied and educational aspects. At the end of the physical and isolated healing process, the neophyte would reemerge into the community with new expectations upon them within the community, reflecting their changes in status from child to marriageable adult.

Since the elements of rites of passage that involve genital modification—particularly those involving girls—have and continue to receive considerable attention from activists and scholars, this chapter begins with an overview of rites of passage generally, then considers published material on those African rituals that involve genital cutting specifically, before framing this research project within the disrupted ritual environment caused by flight from Somalia and resettlement in the United States.

Rituals of Identity Construction

Rituals to mark a shift in identity during the life course, or rites of passage, have long been the subject of considerable ethnographic interest and folkloristic analysis, particularly those celebrated in an African context. From their earliest appearance, however, consideration of a ritual's specifics and their symbolic interpretation has overshadowed analysis of the construction of identity that results from participation in that ritual. One of the earliest studies was a nineteenth-century folkloristic project of classifying rituals based on external similarities, which inspired Arnold van Gennep to propose a new approach to ritual based on ceremonial patterns. In his now-classic work, *The Rites of Passage* ([1909] 1960, 6), van Gennep worked from contemporary ethnographic literature, including Weule's descriptions of initiation ritual among the Yao in East Africa, one of the ancestral forebears of the present-day Somali Bantu (Weule and Werner 1909). Through his study of this literature, van Gennep observed a common tripartite pattern within the ceremonies that he described as rites of passage. Working first from passages through territory, and then through dwellings, he noted that all passages, and the rites that mark them, consist of an ongoing process of separation, transition, and incorporation (van Gennep [1909] 1960, 10–11). While his book considers all life-cycle events, the tripartite characterization is acknowledged as his central contribution to the field. In fact, the work is more complex than the tripartite ritual analysis, and considers the significance of puberty itself as a developmental milestone in initiation ritual. Van Gennep argued that, while puberty's various physiological manifestations often serve as a harbinger for this internal transition to adulthood within the life course, the ritual, despite its common link to body modifications like genital cutting, ultimately served to differentiate one group from its neighbors, in contrast to suggestions that it was tied to new, pubescent powers of sexuality ([1909] 1960, 73–74). In other words, while van Gennep's work was definitive in that it demonstrated a consistent ceremonial pattern—particularly in initiation ritual— it also noted that these rites define social identity, placing an individual within a particular group (adult males and females) and excluding the individual from other groups (children and the opposite gender).

It was, however, based on the ethnographic fieldwork of others, so while it offers a broad understanding of an important phenomenon, it is limited in its depth. That kind of analysis would come a half century later from Victor Turner, who further elaborated van Gennep's structure based on his research among the Ndembu, a Bantu-speaking group from Zambia. Turner defined the rites of passage by their transitions between states—culturally recognized, stable conditions—through a transitional phase characterized by its processural nature. In this liminal stage, the initiate becomes a different being, no longer classified and not yet classified (Turner 1967, 94, 96). Turner, also working from the considerable influence of Freud (Oring 1993, 275), provided numerous illustrations of the symbolic elements of Ndembu initiation ritual and insightful analysis of social relations during the phase, all of which have become paradigmatic in academic analysis of liminality and rites of passage. However, for my purposes, his discussion of the ultimate purpose of the initiation ritual is more significant. Quoting from Richards's (1956) work in Mozambique—one of the few accounts of female initiation ritual in the 1930s—Turner notes that the local name of their initiation ritual illustrates the community understanding of growing a girl, or effecting "an ontological transformation" during initiation (1967, 102). The liminal space, he argues, provides for "the esoteric teaching which grows girls and makes men. . . . The arcane knowledge or 'gnosis' obtained in the liminal period is felt to change the inmost nature of the neophyte, impressing him, as a seal impresses wax, with the characteristics of his new state. It is not a mere acquisition of knowledge, but a change in being" (102). I want to emphasize this shift in identity from the start of this discussion simply because it points to a common disparity in emphasis between those undergoing an initiation ritual and those analyzing it from outside the group. As a result, it has been difficult to find common understanding, particularly when those rituals are controversial to outsiders who seek to influence their practice.

The centrality of this shift in beingness is at the center of the work of one of Turner's contemporaries, religious studies scholar Mircea Eliade. Rather than concentrate on the symbolic or structural elements of ritual events, he highlighted the transformative effects of initiation ritual on individuals, pointing out that these rituals imprint the stamp of culture onto community members, thereby defining what it is to be human. Although his language is ethnocentric, he grasped the fundamental importance of initiation ritual within groups that practice it, pointing out that "for archaic thought, then, man is *made*—he does not make himself all by himself. It is the old initiates, the spiritual masters, who make him" (Eliade 1965, xiv). Put simply, ritual events create a new social identity for the initiate, one that connects him or her to the community as a new person through the experience of ordeals and the acquisition of sacred knowledge, including the appropriate behavior for adults within social institutions, and the myths and traditions of the group related to aspects of the divine (x). Like van Gennep, Eliade worked from the ethnographies of other scholars to make his most specific conclusions, which highlight his focus on the religious elements of the ritual. His central argument, however, underscores the transformative, identity-shifting effects of initiation rites. Among ethnographers, however, the identity-shifting elements of initiation rituals have often been lost in the details of the ritual event. Turner and the ritual scholars who have followed him have produced a large body of compelling ethnographic descriptions and solid theoretical analysis of specific initiation rituals, but these scholars often place very little emphasis on the long-term impact on initiates as members of a community, which is crucial to understanding their importance within the groups that practice them.

Nearly two decades after Turner, Pierre Bourdieu attempted to move away from Turner's highly influential interpretive approach to rites of passage and refocus analysis on the question of boundary creation. In an essay based both on his experience of elite French educational systems and his research among the Kabyle in Algeria, Bourdieu acknowledged the contributions of van Gennep and Turner but noted that their work does little more than name and describe rituals of passage. He argued that the passage itself is less interesting than the "social significance of the line, the boundary, whose crossing, whose transgression, the ritual renders legitimate" (Bourdieu [1982] 1992, 80). The important result of the rite, he argued, is not so much to differentiate some members of the community from others (e.g., boys vs. men), but members of one community from members of another (e.g., Kikuyu vs. Luo). As a result, he suggested that the rites are important not for the passage of the individual but because they are rites of institution for the community. In other words, these rites legitimize what to outsiders seems to be an arbitrary boundary but which the community represents as legitimate and natural. Addressing the question of identity, he wrote that the "institution of an identity . . . is the imposition of a social essence. The process of institution, the assigning of an essence, a competence, is the imposition of a right to be, which is at the same time the imposition of an expectation and even a duty to be, something" (83). In this framework, the traditional initiation ritual not only creates a new member with adult privileges in the community but also imposes the responsibility of adulthood upon the initiate (80–86).

The theme that emerges in this brief consideration of literature on rites of passage generally also echoes in analysis specifically on rites of passage involving genital cutting. While the individual aspects of initiation rituals are often the subject of scrutiny and interpretation by outsiders, to the initiate and the community practicing those rituals, the rite of passage is most important in that it constructs a boundary that imposes a new social identity and constructs a responsibility to the community on the newly initiated. This approach to becoming an adult requires them to conform to their new roles as men or women within the community. As we move to consider the literature on rites of passage involving genital cutting specifically, the fundamental purpose of these rites tends to become even further lost in controversy over individual aspects of the rituals as well as their interpretation by outsiders. As this chapter moves into a discussion of the specifics of practice, I caution the reader to keep in mind the fundamental importance of the identity shift, as the practices cannot be understood in isolation from their purpose within the group practicing them.

Rites of Passage Involving Genital Modification

Much of what is commonly known about rites of passage involving genital cutting focuses on the practices that affect females. However, it is important to note that, in groups that engage in it, genital cutting generally is part of the rite of passage for both genders. Consequently, this discussion will begin by describing the physical elements of the ritual for males before moving into the more controversial practices involving females. Since the preceding discussion summarized the larger context in which these practices occur, I will concentrate at this point on what happens to the bodies of initiates in order to establish a common understanding for the discussion that follows.

For male initiates, the traditional genital cutting ritual typically involves circumcision, that is, the removal of some, or all, of the foreskin (prepuce) of the penis. A recent report by the World Health Organization (WHO) and Joint United Nations Programme on HIV/AIDS notes that circumcision has been practiced as a part of the rites of passage into adulthood by various ethnic groups in sub-Saharan Africa for millennia (HIV/AIDS 2007, 4). Given the variable nature of the practice among diverse groups and within a variety of contexts in sub-Saharan Africa, the WHO/UN Report relies on the details provided in specific studies rather than attempting to estimate the number of groups engaging in the practice across the continent. In the nonclinical, ritual practices it is able to document among certain Bantu-speaking groups, there is a consistent pattern. Typically, the circumciser pulls the foreskin away from the shaft of the penis and then uses a penknife or razor blade to remove some of the foreskin without anesthesia. Because the event generally takes place within groups, these instruments often are used repeatedly without any kind of sterilization technique. The wound is then dressed with natural healing salve, such as eucalyptus leaves or maize, for the duration of the healing period when the initiates remain secluded (9). Although the WHO supports the practice of male circumcision generally, it notes that these nonclinical practices have the potential for adverse medical effects, including the need for further corrective procedures due to the partial removal of the foreskin, gangrene, irreversible damage to the penis and urinary tract, ongoing penile pain, keloid scarring, septicemia and other infections, hemorrhage, and death (20).

Even greater controversy and caution surrounds practices involving female genital cutting (FGC). In general, despite wide variety in practice, scholars and advocates in this subject categorize four general types of FGC, which range from the mild to the severe. The first, known as *sunna* in reference to Islamic tradition urging groups that practice FGC to exercise moderation, typically involves a pricking of the clitoris in a manner that does not result in a permanent wound (Hernlund and Shell-Duncan 2007, 20). In the general typology originally adopted by the WHO in 1995 and later modified to account for the many variables in practice, *sunna* is classified as Type IV, a grouping of unclassified practices involving the female genitalia that do not result in permanent alteration. In contrast, Type I, generally referred to as clitoridectomy, involves removal of the external clitoris in whole or part. Type II, generally referred to as excision, involves the removal of the labia minora and may include the removal of the external elements of the clitoris and labia majora. Type III, generally referred to as infibulation, involves the creation of a seal covering part of the vaginal orifice, generally through the stitching together of the labia minora or labia majora. This type may also involve the removal of the external clitoris and labia minora (World Health Organization 2008, 24). From this point, rather than use the typology, I will typically refer to the specific practices as *sunna*, clitoridectomy, excision, or infibulation, as these are the clearest terms for understanding the actual procedure performed on the initiate. Like the procedures carried out on boys, FGC is often conducted without anesthesia, using unsophisticated implements, limited antiseptics, and natural healing salves, and therefore carries all the same potential for adverse outcomes as those noted about ritual circumcision of boys. In addition to the outcomes listed above, WHO notes that because infibulation is of longer duration and more extensive physically, females who undergo it face greater trauma and a longer healing period. Likewise, infibulation affects access to the vaginal canal in the long term, so unlike the experience of the boys, both sexual intercourse and childbirth are inescapably affected by the procedure, which may require additional genital cutting for the girls to participate in both activities (World Health Organization 2008, 34–35). Later in the chapter, I will discuss ongoing research on the impact clitoridectomy, excision, and infibulation have on women's ability to experience orgasm, as the emerging research suggests that its effects are variable rather than absolute.

However, at this point, it is important to acknowledge that the controversial nature of FGC has resulted in considerable attention paid to this subject over time from both inside and outside the communities that practice it. During the colonial period in East Africa, Europeans attempted to eliminate the practice but met with considerable indigenous resistance (Berman and Lonsdale 1992; Thomas 2003). By the 1980s the eradication of FGC again became a focus, this time by feminist advocates of abolition (Abdalla 1982; Dorkenoo 1994; Lightfoot-Klein 1989), whose work drew the attention of the global community to these practices. However, this public attention did not immediately result in empirical research on the subject. In fact, in her review of the literature available up to 1996, medical anthropologist Carla Makhlouf Obermeyer acknowledged that the published materials in French and English were "long on advocacy and short on empirically based research" (1999, 85), noting that many of the claims of prevalence and health effects—which made up only 10 percent of the sources she found on the subject—often relied on problematic data. Since then, increasing effort has gone into gathering data on prevalence and effects of FGC, while much of the popular discussion remains heavily influenced by efforts to eradicate the practice and interpret it, but with limited effort to understand the indigenous reasoning behind it.

At the same time, cultural analysts have remained fairly consistent in their interpretation of the practice of genital cutting in African communities. Within that context, there is a general scholarly consensus that the purpose of such cutting is to construct gender on what were previously perceived as hermaphroditic children, thereby creating gendered males and females through body modification. By removing the foreskin of the penis, which is most analogous to the labia, and removing the clitoris, which is most analogous to the penis, African communities construct gender on their initiates (Ahmadu 2007; Beidelman 1991; Berman and Lonsdale 1992; Boddy 2007; Thomas 2003; Zabus 2008). To elaborate, Ahmadu (2000) points out that, among the Kono of Sierra Leone—who practice excision—the natural body is not the one girls are born with, but the one that is constructed socially. It is worth noting how this corresponds to Richards's and Eliade's earlier analysis, that initiation ritual demonstrates how communities make adults; individuals do not arrive at adulthood on their own.

While Africanist scholarship agrees that the construction of gender through genital alteration moves male and female individuals forward in the life cycle, scholars have disagreed as to whether FGC confers adulthood on the girls. In her early ethnography, Richards noted that female Bemba initiates have already helped with babies and experimented with sex before their initiation, so the point of the event is to learn secret terms and songs, the secret language of marriage, and the sequence of the rites, while reaffirming the obligations women will have in marriage. By participating in the rite of passage, the girls acquire the right to bear a child, which may not involve an elevation of status but does result in a new role (Richards 1956, 125–29). This corresponds with Boddy's analysis some fifty years later, that the experience of infibulation among Hofriyati girls is "indispensible to becoming marriageable, a full adult *normal*" (2007, 51). This understanding seems in contrast with that of Ahmadu, who emphasizes power over marriageability in her discussion of the rite, noting that through excision, Kono women separate themselves from masculinity and construct matriarchal power (2007, 308), and Declich, whose work on matrikin groups and their rituals among southern Somali agriculturalists in the 1980s ties ritual performance directly to the construction and perpetuation of female authority (1995a, 1995b).

Regardless of whether female initiates attain adulthood or simply marriage-ability from the rite of passage, passage through it enhances their status in the life cycle. Boddy notes that, while the alterations made to the female body de-emphasize sexuality, they enhance her potential for exercising fertility, which is the path to advancing her position in the Hofriyati community by giving birth (Boddy 1989, 687). Put simply, in this worldview, power comes not from sexuality but from fertility, and by undergoing the process of infibulation, a girl launches herself as a fertile being with the potential to create a lineage section. This is the source of her power, rather than through her prowess as a sexual partner (53). It is these differing approaches to understanding power between African com-munities that practice it and feminist advocates of abolition, argues Lyons, that have created an impasse in discussions about the practice of female genital cutting (Lyons 2007).

To recap, regardless of the extent to which female initiates emerge as adults or as candidates for marriage with no immediate elevation in status, there seems to be a general agreement among most scholars that genital cutting rituals construct gender within African communities that practice them, and that FGC in particular is significant to the community in the role it plays in affecting the ability of a young woman to marry within the community. In chapter 4, I will take up a discussion about the impact transnational migration is having on the practice and how that relates to this question of marriageability. However, it is important at this juncture to acknowledge the distinction between how the practice is justified within those communities that practice it compared to the perspective of those who seek its abolition, where much of the criticism surrounding FGC focuses on its long-term impact to health and sexuality. In her analysis of Western feminist responses to the practice, Harriet D. Lyons has noted that feminist analysis of the practice, which has informed much of the popular literature on eradication, has itself been deeply influenced by Freud and the Western feminist reaction to him. As a result, she argues, it is inevitable that the practice would be largely interpreted by Western feminists as a particularly insidious effort by male hierarchy to dominate women through sexual subjugation (Lyons 2007). What she is referring to specifically is that Sigmund Freud theorized that the central milestone of puberty is that it establishes the sexual primacy of the genitalia. For boys, puberty makes penetration by the penis the central aim of sexual stimulation, while for girls puberty begins a process of transferring clitoral stimulation (common during childhood) to other vaginal orifices requiring stimulation through penetration (Freud, Strachey, and Freud [1905] 1953, 221–22). This specific Freudian idea, that clitoral stimulation is a passage in sexual development that becomes insignificant with the passage to adulthood, essentially posits that the process of human development universally involves a clitoridectomy of sorts, regardless of specific cultural practice. While Freud's idea is highly contested at this point, its existence demonstrates how Western approaches to sexuality—feminist or not—have also been shaped by the historical and cultural context in which they develop, and they shape Western reactions to non-Western approaches to the body and sexuality.

In fact, the cultural and anatomical realities of sexual practice are both much more complex. As there are in many aspects of culture, the difference between traditional African and modernist Western understandings of the purpose and practice of sexuality is noteworthy. In a cogent and forceful effort to illustrate this, Boddy points out that the Western notion that rights and social identity reside in the appetites and pleasures of an individual body is in conflict with African ideas in which the person is understood in relational terms (2007, 62). The practice of sexuality ultimately comes down to cultural understandings of what is considered natural for a human being. In the modernist West, the individual ideally exercises autonomy, particularly in regard to her own body and sexuality. This explains why there is general condemnation of FGC practices, which are perceived as an irreversible imposition on an individual—typically a child—by adult others, while at the same time, cosmetic surgeries and other medical interventions that modify the natural body of an adult in an effort to enhance sexual attractiveness and pleasure are not prohibited in law and may even be covered by health insurance. However, if one views the natural state of personhood in relational instead of individual terms, then the failure to attain the condition of marriageability is the most unnatural state, as it could impede one's progress toward having legitimate children and thereby attaining greater status, which is why young women within communities of practice will often resist all efforts to eradicate rites of passage involving FGC (Boddy 2007; Thomas 2003; Zabus 2008). If nothing else, this discussion should make clear that FGC is a single element of a larger cultural understanding about the role of sex, which highlights why the abolition of it is complex and problematic.

Incidentally, the potential and experience of orgasm follows this same trajectory of interpretation. If the role of sexuality is tied to the desires and choices of the individual, then it follows that gratification through orgasm is a fundamental goal, or as Lyons notes drily, a moral duty to give and receive (Lyons 2007). With that perspective in mind, then it is obvious that the removal of the external clitoris, perceived to be a central locus of sexual pleasure for women, results in irreparable harm to the quality of the lives of those affected. However, the research on the sexual experience of women who have undergone FGC indicates that the reality is far more complex than what appears on the anatomical surface, and may point once again to the centrality of relationship in determining sexual satisfaction. As both a scholar and as an initiated female member of Kono society, Ahmadu argues forcefully that the experience of excision has not impacted her ability to enjoy sex, something she experienced before and after the procedure. She speculates that this is because only a fraction of the clitoral nerve endings are in the external clitoris; consequently, excision does not damage the extensive remains of the clitoris and its nerve endings beneath the vaginal surface (Ahmadu 2000, 305). In a later study based on interviews with African women who have undergone excision, she argues that the likelihood or failure to achieve orgasm is unrelated to an external clitoris (Ahmadu 2007). In fact, her conclusions correlate to other studies of the experience of orgasm among women who have undergone genital cutting. Based on her interviews with Eritrean women who have been infibulated and Eritrean men who have had sexual intercourse with excised and infibulated women, Dopico points out that most of her subjects report experiences of orgasm despite the modifications made to female genitalia by these procedures. Further, she notes that a variety of factors influence whether sex is enjoyable or not, including sociocultural upbringing, sex-role expectations, one's understanding of the purpose of sex, the relationship with the partner outside the sexual act, and the status of the relationship (Dopico 2007). Johansen comes to many of the same conclusions based on her studies of male and female Somalis living in Norway. Relying on interviews, focus groups, and participant observation, Johansen (2007) concludes that the loss or reduction of the clitoris is not the only issue involved in experiencing orgasm, as both male and female Somalis describe a variety of experiences with sexual responsiveness and pleasure among infibulated women. It is worth noting that research into the effects of FGC on sexual experience is emerging, just as research into health effects is emerging. However, the trend in the current research seems to indicate that, for both women who have undergone FGC and those who have not, the experience of orgasm is based on a number of complex social, cultural, and individual factors, including the state of the relationship. In her conclusion, Dopico argues that there is no uniform expression of sexual behaviors or beliefs because "cultural values dictate the meaning of sexuality, the construction of a normal, healthy, or adequate sexual relationship, and the perception and meaning of sexual satisfaction" (2007, 246). My point in including this research is to note that ultimately, the relational approach to sexuality that is inscribed on the genitalia of African initiates does not seem to inherently preclude individual gratification by women whose genitalia have been modified by it.

My aim in the preceding portions of this chapter is not to settle any kind of debate about genital cutting, its abolition, or its effects, other than to note the value of empirical research on the subject. Rather, my aim has been to provide some background on the model of attaining adult identity through a rite of passage, and to summarize the research on both rites of passage generally and genital cutting specifically, since this model is the most familiar one in the Somali Bantu community undergoing resettlement that I studied. In her highly regarded work on young Sudanese men in resettlement, Felicia McMahon hits upon the problematic nature of a generation of African children who have grown up in refugee camps or in the United States and have not been initiated. As a result of dislocation, their understanding of expressive culture is limited to what is commonly performed by children. Yet, despite the opportunities of globalization and the range of Western products and expressive forms available to them in resettlement, the expressive traditions of their home cultures remain significant for identity construction (McMahon 2007). Mary Bucholtz (2002) has noted young people are not cultural problems for adults to solve but agents of cultural change in their own right, and that they manifest this agency in the everyday. My aim in subsequent chapters is to explore the specifics of how young refugees act as cultural agents in their homes, schools, and ritual lives.

3

Feminine and Masculine on Display

Media Consumption and Gender Models

As noted in chapter 1, the television commands a central place in the living rooms of most Somali Bantu apartments in the United States, and is often—depending on the means of the family—ensconced in an entertainment center with multiple items of entertainment technology: stereo consoles and speakers, DVD players, video cassette recorders, other televisions, and an assortment of music CDs, videotapes, and DVDs. This seeming wealth of media commodities is in sharp contrast to the traditional African décor in the rest of the living space and its corresponding sense of resistance to the external American environment. The contrast is made even sharper when the television (or multiple televisions) remain switched on continuously, broadcasting the sounds of U.S. programs over those of the family gathering in the otherwise African space. As it is for many American families, the entertainment center is an important source of family recreation for Somali Bantu refugees, for whom this access to media is an important new element of family life in resettlement.

The consumption of mediated entertainment is also representative of wider forces affecting diverse culture groups across the globe at the early part of the twenty-first century. Arjun Appadurai argues that two defining characteristics of the postmodern world are the increased scale of human migration across the globe and the abundance of electronic media options available to consumers. These two forces are particularly important, he argues, because they influence the social imagination and, consequently, reshape personal and cultural identity (1996, 3–4). In addition, Lila Abu-Lughod notes that while contemporary culture is coproduced by both local and mass media forces that cross national boundaries, global media is still ultimately mixed up with the local and its meaning systems (1997, 121–23). To Appadurai, the influence of mass media on young refugees is particularly significant because diverse media choices offer young people a multiplicity of alternatives to the models of adulthood provided by

Media center in a Somali Bantu home, ca. 2008. Photo by author.

parents or elders in traditional practices of cultural reproduction (1996, 43–45). In order to explore this larger question of how media consumption affects practices of cultural reproduction in a transnational context, this chapter explores the media practices of the teenage Somali Bantu refugees at Wedgewood Village and its didactic role as they acquire an understanding of what it is to be adult, gendered members of an ethnic community when all of these identities are in flux.

As noted in the previous chapter, the living room is a space dominated by women, the site of much of their labor and entertainment. Consequently, women have considerable authority about the media choices made in that space and are its primary consumers. While women, teen girls, and young children sit in the room and watch the television, they also prepare food and care for the gathered children. Meanwhile, Somali Bantu men and teen boys move in and out of the room, engaging briefly in the ongoing television entertainment, then typically move on to other activities, including backstage media consumption with their peers. With the disruption of traditional rites of passage, particularly the extended liminal space that allows for the transmission of knowledge about gender identity by elders to initiates, it is in these media encounters where young people are often explicitly exposed to distinct gendered models of adulthood. For Somali Bantu teen girls, the viewing of African-made drama, primarily involving family/communal crisis, makes up a significant proportion of their media engagement and is typically consumed within the extended family structure in the public social space of the living room. Likewise, for Somali Bantu teen boys, the viewing of physical competition, primarily contests of World Wrestling Entertainment (WWE), make up a significant proportion of their media engagement. Unlike the viewing of African dramas, WWE activities are typically removed to a gender-segregated space, often a bedroom, where access is limited to teenage males. In addition, even outside the secluded confines of gendered domestic space, the buying and trading of consumer products related to the WWE are significant and exclusively male activities. Among Somali Bantu teenagers, communal television viewing has become an important avenue for reinforcing traditionally held values about gender roles and domestic life, while also exposing them to U.S. models of gender and product consumption.

Video Watching as Cultural Process

Because the living room of the family apartment is the center of domestic life, Somali Bantu girls most often engage in media consumption in that space, in the company of female elders. Within this family context, their viewing is dominated by African-made videos, primarily dramas involving family/communal crisis. Available on video cassette and DVD, the production of these video dramas has escalated in Africa over the last decade, beginning first in Nigeria (which has become known as Nollywood for its volume of production) and moving out into other African countries as the availability of video technology has made it easier for local filmmakers to create and distribute their own works. The cheap production and distribution of videos has also made it easy for increasingly larger numbers of Africans to view and circulate these movies, even in diaspora. John McCall notes that while celluloid films were not largely accessible to African audiences, video production has made locally produced videos into an astonishingly familiar form of entertainment, because their content reflects contemporary African concerns, they contain familiar aesthetic markers, and they are easily shared in family groups. Not only are the videos popular, he notes, but they have also established themselves as a forum for public discourse because they raise larger social issues often overlooked by the more highbrow film industry (McCall 2002, 80–82, 85).

This element of public discourse is central to the role of videos in transmitting traditional patterns of gender to young refugees resettling into a world both geographically and culturally distant from that of the African continent. Keyan Tomaselli, Arnold Shepperson, and Maureen Eke note that oral traditions, unlike textual ones, require the formation of identity within communal relations, arguing that "oral traditions rely on the contact between generations for the elaboration of individual subjectivities" (1999, 57). In other words, storytelling events and video watching, particularly in a family context, invite multigenerational discussion on content, which in turn shapes the formation of cultural identity. In this instance, movies serve as an extension of local, oral traditions and provide a necessary tool for illiterate families to illustrate traditional social roles for their dislocated children. Jonathan Haynes has noted that, even in Africa, video viewing has become an emergent part of African cultural processes, "producing specifically shaped public spheres as organs for the evolution of specifically African modernities" (2000, 28). In other words, video movies allow African communities to represent modern social problems while they also provide a forum for discussing them. Among resettled Somali Bantu refugees, this pattern of media consumption is not only an evolving cultural process but is also emerging into a cultural routine, which David Lancy describes as a socially created routine used for raising children and inculcating social values (1996, 24). In a more traditional context, games or riddling practices serve as cultural routines, allowing a child to develop cultural identity through play. Among these refugees, the routine viewing of video dramas—particularly those set in an imagined traditional past—perform a similar function. Dislocated as they are, with formal structures of child development in disarray, the family viewing of African videos has become an important, easily repeated routine that allows senior women to reinforce cultural identity for younger ones.

Among the Somali Bantu, African films are a staple of entertainment within the home, garnering greater attention than their American counterparts and often played repeatedly within family gatherings. Since there are, at this point, no professionally produced videos using af-Maay or dramatizing narratives of the Somali Bantu experience, these Nollywood videos provide a way for Somali Bantu refugees to connect with some aspects of traditional African life and culture, despite their settings within other culture groups or an unrelated historical past. In most of my unscheduled visits to Wedgewood, the more senior women were typically tuned into an assortment of such movies set in a premodernist African past, where actors are costumed in traditional dress, sporting furs, beads, and brightly colored African textiles. In most cases, the movie had been seen repeatedly by both the adults and children in the house, who could repeat dialogue from it verbatim and often talked with me over the noise of the television. As I gained greater familiarity with the community, it became increasingly clear that girls were more likely to participate in family viewing of these movies and could offer some synopses of their stories. By contrast, the teenage boys were rarely seen watching these historical dramas, and typically left the living room space to seek entertainment elsewhere while these films occupied the television and others' attention.

At the Movies

In order to describe the experience of these videos within refugee life, I will describe one particular viewing of such a movie within a Somali Bantu family at Wedgewood. I have chosen this specific instance because, on this occasion, the videotape was put on while I was visiting with a wide range of family members, allowing me both to participate in the viewing for an extended period and to observe the practices of the family over the course of most of the film. This visit was scheduled during the summer break from school, and when I arrived, I encountered the middle-aged matriarch, Basra, and members of her extensive family gathering to watch a DVD of a 2007 Nigerian movie, *Stronger than Pain*, which won best acting awards for both its male and female lead at the

2008 Africa Movie Academy Awards. In this instance, the family's lower television was turned off while a multigenerational collection of women gathered
in the sitting room to watch the film, chat, and care for about a dozen children
ranging in age from one to ten. For parts of the movie, we were joined by Basra's
husband, Abuukar, but never by any boys over the age of ten. Also, Basra and
two of her married daughters were engaged throughout the movie in a game of
cards that further caused them to divide their attention between the film and
the children surrounding them.

Like many of the films I encountered during home visits, *Stronger than Pain* is
set in a rural village sometime in an imagined African traditional past. The
male characters routinely wear two pieces of woven cloth, one wrapped around
the waist and another held in place at the shoulder, and the women wear ensembles of cloths dyed with traditional designs and tied onto their bodies to
reveal bare midriffs and most of their legs and arms. Members of both genders
sport a variety of beads, the men wearing theirs around their necks and the
women in their hair and around necks and arms as the costumes allow. Both
males and females have painted decorations on their arms, and the women also
have painted decorations on their faces. Frances Harding notes that characterization in Nigerian movies is often by stereotype, and clothing is typically important for indicating character (2003, 82). With its use of traditional cloths,
beads, and body paint, the costuming and makeup in this case was designed to
evoke a sense of the past. However, the strategic covering of breasts and groins
while revealing midriffs and legs displayed the clothing and modesty standards
of a more modernized Africa. For the Somali Bantu women viewers, who typically cover themselves from head to foot to conform with Islamic standards of
modesty, the fictional village landscape and characters served as a realistic
enough reflection of African life for them to connect with the film while, at the
same time, it was clearly not representative of their own specific cultural history.
Although this is not universally the case with Nigerian videos, this one was in
English, a language that most Somali Bantu adult women who do not work
outside the home struggle to understand. However, most of the women gathered
in Basra's living room had seen the movie so many times that they had the
dialogue memorized, and seemed to have no difficulty understanding the turns
of the plot, despite the language difference and the ongoing card game. In fact,
in an effort to verify that I could understand it, Basra's married daughter,
Aasiya, sat close by me and helpfully narrated the English dialogue to me
throughout the movie, despite the fact that English is my native language.

The film begins with a married couple, Eringa and Ulonna, asleep in bed.
The wife, Eringa, wakes up and eagerly drinks from a gourd only to spit out its

contents upon tasting them. She confronts her sleeping husband and learns that he has replaced her palm wine with water because "a good woman" does not drink early in the morning. She responds by telling him he is "such a weakling." This opening pattern between the couple, of Ulonna attempting to train Eringa into socially acceptable womanhood, and her frustration with his lack of masculine strength, is the core issue of the movie, which essentially maps how this transgressive domestic situation, in which the gender roles are skewed so that the woman displays authority over her husband, causes escalating problems in the wider social hierarchies of African life. The conflict between Ulonna and Eringa soon ripples outside their home. We learn from Ulonna's sister that the village does not approve of Eringa's treatment of him. In response, Ulonna confesses that their sexual chemistry together is unlike what he has experienced with other women, and he believes that this is love, so he has no complaint. His sister, Ure, and her husband, Okolo, question if it is merely weakness. Back at his home, Ulonna and Eringa reconcile and are sexually intimate. In subsequent scenes, his agemates counsel him to find a new wife, reminding him that "warriors [Ulonna's current status in the life cycle] are never scared of their wives." Eringa finds him and scolds him publicly, and at home nothing he does satisfies her. She continues to scold and hit him, then demands that he make love to her. He refuses, asking for respect. She insists that she too is only asking for respect. When she tries to force him to function sexually, he insists that he is not a donkey, and again flees to his family. Later, other women of Eringa's age group come to confront her. They plan to chase her out of the village for being a bad wife, ending the marriage and ostracizing her. But Ulonna stops them, insisting that hurting him is a way of showing affection and that he has no complaint against his wife. His sister and her husband then enlist an unmarried village beauty to try and seduce him away, offering him to her in marriage. Soon, there is another domestic quarrel over the dinner that Ulonna has made, followed by another confrontation between Eringa and her agemates. When Ulonna takes Eringa's side against his sister, Ure tells him to stop coming to her home to cry and hide from his wife. The would-be seductress then makes her move, and Ulonna is caught embracing her. He runs and tries to hide at his sister's, who sends him home. Eringa appears to forgive him, and he tells her that "every man does one foolish thing every day of his life." Once he falls asleep, however, Eringa brings out a whip and beats him with it. After this altercation, the elders come and tell Ulonna that Eringa must leave the village, or they will drag her into the bush, rape her, and leave her there alone. Ulonna protests, telling them his love is stronger than pain, but Eringa flees to her parents' house outside Ulonna's village.

In the second part, Eringa returns to the village, and she is seen. So the warriors follow her back to her parents' home and beat her unconscious. Ulonna nurses her back to health, and while he is caring for her, the elders come and order Ulonna away from her. He gets a knife and begins a fight, so they leave. At this point, Eringa becomes a loving wife, apologizing to Ulonna and telling him how lucky she is to have him, and he promises to stay by her side. The elders return and threaten him with ostracism for his disobedience to them and for living at his wife's father's house when she has been ostracized by the village. He tells them they cannot disown him because they do not own him in the first place. The elders leave, and Eringa suggests that Ulonna leave her, but he stays. When he appeals to his sister for help caring for Eringa, he is rebuffed. When he returns to Eringa, she gets on her knees and apologizes, saying she will stay by him and be a good wife. He sings and cries. When Ulonna appeals to a village elder to allow her to return because of her changed personality, the elder throws him out and Ulonna insults him. Upon returning to Eringa, she suggests that they stay at her place, but Ulonna wants to be in his father's compound. Eringa then makes him a delicious soup, and they share this meal and are happy. Soon, the warriors from his village come to the compound with elders and knives to destroy the house of her father. Eringa runs away and tries to eat poisoned leaves, but Ulonna stops her. They return to Ulonna's house in the village, and the elders and warriors soon come to kill them. Ulonna confronts them, tying a noose around Eringa's neck and asking for permission to hang her along with himself. They plead with him to marry a good woman, and he reminds them that nobody is perfect, telling them if they can produce a perfect woman to marry, he will kill Eringa and do so. In the meantime, he insists that he loves her. The head warrior lays down his stick and leaves, and soon all of the men from the village go. Eringa and Ulonna return to the house, where she immediately begins bullying and insulting him. He laughs very hard and tells her he loves her but that she has started her nagging too soon. As the film ends, he embraces her, laughing while she scowls (Chikere 2007).

Despite its melodrama and setting within a romanticized African past, *Stronger than Pain* highlights two important African themes that resonate deeply within the community of refugees living in a dislocated present: gender roles within domestic life, and the hierarchies of authority within the larger community and their control over the individual. This theme is not particular to this film, and according to most synopses offered to me of other African movies, the conflict between the demands of leaders and the problematic love of individuals often leads to violence and despair in these dramas as well. In her essay on what she describes as the "woman-on-top" phenomenon, Natalie Zemon Davis describes a similar reaction to domineering wives within early modern European communities, noting that the community often publicly and physically punished the transgressive couple in an effort to restore the traditional hierarchy within the home (1975, 140). While, on one level, this particular movie consistently demonstrates the importance of male authority over women, community authority over the individual, and elder authority over their juniors, these hierarchies are also continually subverted throughout the story: Eringa bosses Ulonna, their agemates are not able to force them into social conformity, and the elders do not ultimately get their way. In the end, the question of both village and domestic long-term harmony is left unresolved as Eringa has clearly not changed her ways, so more conflict is sure to ensue.

Themes and the Learning of Gender Roles

Because of the film's ambiguity, its interplay of traditional authority and the subversion of it, and the way it asserts good and bad gender roles, watching *Stronger than Pain* in this refugee context provides an interesting focus for examining the development of the social imagination within this particular family and its teens, and how the everyday cultural routine of sharing a video aids elders in shaping adult gender roles among their young members. Harding points out that the watching of videos in family groups allows for a more "African" viewing style, a participatory one in which the viewer argues with and reacts to what happens on screen (2003, 83). In short, it allows for public discourse. As already noted, this film was well known within Basra's family on the day we viewed it. Consequently, family members could divide their attention, and frequently listened for the parts of the movie that particularly resonated with them, thereby reinforcing the importance of those plot turns and lines of dialogue by directing my attention toward the television set, repeating the lines among themselves, laughing and nodding in agreement, and instructing the younger members of the audience. At other points in the movie, when attention was less intense, conversation went on over the video's sound, Abuukar left and returned to the room, and the card game or children garnered greater interest than the drama on screen. Increasingly, what became clear was that the movie had something to teach the adolescent girls about domestic and societal relations, and those points were repeatedly emphasized by elder family members during the shared viewing of the movie.

For the assembled adults, there was no debate about the individual characters of *Stronger than Pain*. Ulonna was a fool, and Eringa needed correcting or removing from the community. In the early part of the story, family members often shook their heads at the inversion of authority within Ulonna's household, making brief sounds of disagreement when Eringa scolded and chased her husband, and shaking their heads in disagreement when Ulonna attempted to justify her behavior. At this stage in the movie, most of the attention of Basra's family members was on the variety of ongoing household activities. Where attention on the video first became highly concentrated was at the point when Eringa demanded that Ulonna make love to her. Ulonna's response, "I am not your donkey," garnered huge laughs from Abuukar and the women gathered in the living room. Although it was delivered on television as an earnest line of dialogue, within the family this dialogue served as a punch line, and was repeated over and over, earning great laughter both from the women and from Abuukar, the sole male in the room. Ulonna's later protestations of innocence when he was caught embracing the young beauty sent to seduce him also elicited comic laughter from all in the group, and most of the adults repeated his dialogue and jumping movement away from the young woman as if it were slapstick. For the assembled group, there was little acceptance of Ulonna's sincerity in either instance. The married women and adult male in the room expected the leading male to desire and perform sex in each scenario, whether with his abusive partner, or with a beautiful young temptress. His protestations that he could not or would not perform sexually when invited to do so were simply absurd. The unmarried young women watching the film, while demonstrating considerably less confidence about the matter, looked to the expertise of the surrounding adults and laughed along with their comedic renderings of the dialogue and action.

As the theme of *Stronger than Pain* became clear, and Ulonna and Eringa continued in their transgressive patterns—she as dominant, he as submissive—the assembled family made it clear that they had little sympathy for either of these characters. Likewise, as the domestic strife spilled outward into the community, moving from Ulonna's kin, to the agemates of the married couple, and eventually to include the elders, the viewers' lack of sympathy turned to contempt. Once the couple onscreen began refusing the authority of the village elders, and as Eringa insulted them, what had been comical became insufferable. The viewers gathered in the living room stopped in their various distractions to shake their heads in righteous anger and make disapproving noises. While initially the pair had been considered foolish, the assembled viewers eventually saw them as deviant, and agreed that both Ulonna and Eringa needed to be ostracized. Meanwhile, in the midst of the collective adult reaction to this issue, the young adults in the room responded very little to the actions onscreen. At the point when Eringa and Ulonna have their first confrontation with the village elders, I asked aloud what I should be learning from the film. Aasiya, a married daughter of the family in her twenties, answered simply, "Be nice." After a few moments of thought, she explained, "I try to be nice with my husband and everyone I meet." As evidence of Eringa's failings as a wife, Basra pointed out, "She treats him poorly and she cannot cook." Abshiro, another of her married daughters, explained to me, "The woman is not a good woman; they have no children, and she cannot cook," providing even further reasons why the marriage should end, particularly since its strife had now spilled over to the surrounding village. In contrast, seventeen-year-old Maryan offered only that Ulonna was foolish, an opinion clearly shared by those gathered around her. As an unmarried teenager, she could not judge Eringa as an experienced wife would, but she learned from the women around her that the standard for judging good women is that they observe existing social hierarchies of age and gender, produce children, and cook good food for their husbands, as Eringa does later in the film when she is repentant.

In an attempt to gather more information, I asked if the kind of disruption caused by Ulonna and Eringa's marriage would happen within their community in Somalia. Aasiya responded quickly that it was happening to the villagers on film because "these are not Muslims." Then, after another moment to gather her thoughts in English, she explained further, "I never argue with my husband. I walk away even when he wants to start a fight." What Islam offers that the fictional village did not, in Aasiya's opinion, is a fixed hierarchy of men over women, a social organization that maintains peace within the household so that domestic conflict does not escalate and disrupt the larger society. Ironically, Aasiya's personal experience is an inversion of the notion that a fixed domestic order maintains a harmonious social order. The larger societal conflict that erupted in Somalia in the early 1990s has, in fact, broken down households and separated families. Ladan Affi has noted the toll that the breakdown of the Somali state has had on marriage and family as institutions. Many women, like Aasiya, are single-parent heads of households, and even when a marriage remains intact, there tends to be a higher incidence of marital conflict over resources just as the social systems for mediating marital conflict—extended clan and family systems—have broken down (2004, 112–13). In this particular case, Aasiya's husband remains in East Africa awaiting the appropriate paperwork to join her in the United States. Their separation, which had lingered for four years at that point, has not only left Aasiya as the successful head of her own household but has also caused her to consider divorce so that she can remarry and have more children while she is still young. But within her mother's home, as we consider the imagined African village and the traditional social hierarchy we see on screen, a pattern of social cohesion remains workable in the social imagination, and it begins with the proper respect of a Muslim wife for her husband; it begins with her effort to be nice.

At the same time, raised exclusively in refugee camps and U.S. housing projects in a family splintered by war and dislocation, Maryan seemed considerably less certain of the importance of social hierarchies and the role of a good wife, offering no lessons to be learned from the video. In her work on a legend cycle involving a transgressive woman in Indiana, Janet Langlois noted a similar difference in opinion between younger and older community members about the importance of rigid gender roles in the narration of the legend. By questioning the gender of the legend's protagonist (a woman accused of murdering her husbands and children), older members of the community highlighted the necessity for clear sexual distinctions in a well-ordered community. Younger narrators never discussed the gender issue, which Langlois attributed to the decline in symbolic power of men's and women's roles in twentieth-century America (1985, 117). The rigid social hierarchies Aasiya underscored were largely absent in the life experience of Maryan, so the one relating to gender was also less certain.

Once the first part of *Stronger than Pain* ended, and Eringa was run out of the village, gathered family members lost interest in the film, and the women began to prepare for the evening meal, at first talking over the movie, then switching it off before its conclusion. They had shown me the important part of the film, which they had been eager for me to view, this representation of African village life, its patterns, and a struggle to rid itself of an unruly woman and correct a weak man. To complete my own picture, I asked Aasiya how the film ends, and she reported that Eringa eventually mocks the village elders because they are old, so their sons come and beat her into a coma. In fact, this is not how the story concludes, but Aasiya's ending restored order to the fictional village and was a satisfying one for her. Community harmony is reestablished with the destruction of the transgressive woman, and the gathered adult viewers considered that a good outcome. Ironically, the lone dissenting voice to this collective female opinion came from the teenage grandson, sixteen-year-old Mahdi, who returned to the house for his dinner and talked with me about the movie, which he, too, had seen before. Mahdi's opinion on the characters in the film differed significantly from those of his elder family members. He demonstrated virtually no interest in Eringa, who had been the source of much scorn by the women family members. Instead, he focused on Ulonna, whom he considered heroic because of his decision to stand by the woman he loves, regardless of who tempts him to leave her. To teenage Mahdi, the larger society was in the wrong, and by sticking with his wife, Ulonna showed exceptional strength. For him, the film was a very satisfying romance, providing a modern model of domestic life rather than reinforcing traditional models of social control.

In his work on the proliferation of Bollywood videos in Nigeria prior to the explosion of the home-grown video industry, Brian Larkin points out that many of those films also focus on the problem of marriage, how its traditional role as the bedrock for stable social life often conflicts with its more modern purpose as the union of two individuals who love each other. He notes that the Indian videos were popular in this African context because they often illustrate "the tension of preserving traditional moral values in a time of profound change" (1997, 413), and therefore epitomize the conflict traditional cultures have with modernity. This instance of viewing *Stronger than Pain*, admittedly an ambiguous film, demonstrates adults' use of video watching in the home to illustrate traditional patterns of African life to young people who have very limited experience with those patterns in Africa. During the family viewing of this film, there was no ambiguity. The young women who remained in the living room were reminded repeatedly that women and men have distinct roles within family life. Men are authoritative figures who are expected to be routinely potent domestically and sexually. Women are subordinate figures who are measured by their acceptance of social hierarchies as well as their ability to cook and reproduce. A disruption to this order results in disruption to the larger social order and should conclude with the removal of the transgressors from the local community. Through repeated multigenerational viewing and shared commentary on these themes, community elders have transformed video viewing into cultural routine in which they inculcate social values and reinforce gender roles for their teenage girls (Lancy 1996).

Teenage Boys and Television Practices

I noted previously that the living rooms of Somali Bantu apartments are dominated by women and that Somali Bantu men and teen boys tend to move in and out of that space, engaging briefly in its activities. In contrast, their consumption of media is often part of a backstage activity with their peers (Goffman 1959). For Somali Bantu teen boys, the viewing of physical competition, primarily contests of World Wrestling Entertainment (WWE), make up a significant proportion of their media engagement. Unlike the viewing of African dramas, WWE activities are typically removed to a gender-segregated space, often a bedroom, where access is limited to teenage males. In addition, even outside the secluded confines of gendered domestic space, the buying and trading of consumer products related to the WWE are significant and exclusively male activities. Among Somali Bantu boys, both viewing practices and media content indicate that the media provides important models of gendered behavior that both reinforce traditional gender roles and connect them to important values within American life and to consumer practices that extend the social imaginary of professional wrestling into their daily lives.

In keeping with this removed practice, my initial exposure to the WWE came not from watching it in the Somali Bantu home but in a discussion with Ibraahin, a teenager I met in school. Not only was this conversation an introduction to an important practice in his peer group but its full context also highlights the significant elements of WWE programming and the ways many boys absorb them as part of their ongoing effort to find models for male adulthood. At that time, Ibraahin's household included his mother and two sisters, one of whom was blind. The responsibility of caring for her disabled daughter prevented Ibraahin's mother from supporting the family financially, and left him with concerns about money and his future potential to provide for himself and his family. Because he had begun to demonstrate seriousness of purpose in his studies, Ibraahin had been enrolled in an after-school trade program at a local community college where he was gaining skills as an electrician. In nearly all of our tutoring sessions, Ibraahin asked me for advice on how to earn an even larger income, whether to continue in high school and attempt to get his diploma and consider attending college, or dedicate himself full time to his trade course instead and progress higher in his electrical certifications. Every now and then, as he explored these pragmatic options with me, Ibraahin would ask me about more fantastic ways to be successful in America. One idea he had, for example, was to go on *American Idol* and, by winning it, become a successful pop star. Although I thought his options to do this were limited by his lack of English-language skills and inexperience performing music of any kind, Ibraahin seemed confident that he could win the competition if he could find somebody to support him with some musical training and help auditioning for the show.

Later, in a similar discussion, Ibraahin asked me a series of questions about the WWE. He had been watching wrestling with his cousin Haaruun, and the two had begun debating whether what they saw on television wrestling was real or staged. Ibraahin insisted it was a performance, while Haaruun thought it was a contest of strength. It is important to note that the relationship between Ibraahin and Haaruun was complicated and symbiotic, particularly in their approaches to integrating into U.S. life. While Ibraahin lived in a household of women and felt considerable pressure as its sole male to support the family, Haaruun had lost his mother and lived a bachelor existence in a second family apartment away from the home of his father's current wife and their children. Neither boy had daily access to an adult Somali Bantu male as a role model, and both were picking pieces from the variety of models around them in their progress toward manhood. After a period of wild behavior and disrespect for school authority, Ibraahin had begun working hard at his education and sought out additional support from teachers to improve his chances at success. Haaruun, on the other hand, barely participated in school. Most efforts to teach him were met with blank stares or laughter. At the housing project where they lived, Haaruun was securing a reputation as a troublemaker because his unique living situation offered him considerable freedom, while it simultaneously failed to meet many of his needs. Both Ibraahin and Haaruun wanted to establish themselves as successful men in Somali Bantu–American life, but they were pursuing very different paths to that end. At the point when Ibraahin asked me about the WWE, he saw a route to the future through hard work at school and the development of an employable skill, while Haaruun was inclined toward petty thieving and found role models in his considerable media consumption. According to Ibraahin, the two argued not only over whether the fights on the WWE were staged but also over Haaruun's plan to become a WWE wrestler when he reached an employable age. Of course, the lure of such models was attractive to Ibraahin as well, and his question to me also indicated that he too would consider a career as a wrestler if I thought it was a feasible way forward.

Watching the WWE

As my fieldwork moved from the school and into individual homes, it became increasingly clear that the WWE was an important element of media consumption for most Somali Bantu teenage boys, and I soon learned that this avid viewing interest also had an impact on the boys' Internet consumption and participation in other competitive activities. Most Somali Bantu teenagers avidly followed one or both of two weekly programs, *Raw* and *Smackdown*. Both of these programs are owned by the WWE, the largest professional wrestling promotion in the world. Professional wrestling as demonstrated on both programs is a combination of three elements: sport spectacle, complex narrative drama, and repeated promotion of other WWE products. To illustrate these three elements, I will describe an episode of *Raw* I watched at Wedgewood in the company of two Somali Bantu teenagers, Hanad and Mahdi. In this particular instance, we began watching the program on a television in the almost empty living room of Hanad's house. Upon my arrival, female members of Hanad's family appeared from other apartments to be introduced to me as a visitor. I want to note that, while many teenage and adult Somali Bantu females claim that they follow the sport, this front-room consumption of it with multiple genders and generations of family members was not common to my experience but was unique to the circumstances of this visit. When the program began, we were joined by Hanad's father, two adult women, and Hanad's younger sister, Haajiro. The adult women left soon after the program began, and while the father stayed, he largely ignored the onscreen activities. Haajiro, like the boys, watched eagerly and sometimes ventured an opinion about one or another character. It was the boys, however, who dominated the discussion of the events on television.

As the program opened, a retired "legend," Ric Flair, was using a microphone to call out Chris Jericho, a younger wrestler with whom he had an established rivalry that had recently spilled over into Flair's retirement. Soon, Jericho interrupted Flair's challenge from a microphone in the backstage area of the stadium, and eventually he appeared in the stadium and approached Flair in the ring. Both men were dressed in gray suits and ties, seemingly unprepared to wrestle, while fans shouted for them to fight. Soon the scripted argument turned into a physical confrontation between the older and younger man, and the narration was taken up by the unseen sports commentators who explained the background of the conflict to uninitiated television viewers. As Jericho punched Flair in the face, pushed him to the ground, and threw him, bleeding, into the stands, the commentators registered their disapproval, noting that Flair is a hall of famer, and Jericho was simply humiliating him. Jericho continued to beat Flair, blood pouring out of him, outside the ring. Eventually, Jericho grabbed a camera off one of the production staff and attacked Flair with it. Flair then collapsed, seemingly unconscious. The crowd roared and chanted, and Jericho stripped Flair of his gold watch and stomped it into the ground as the commentators called out for him to stop. The camera closed in on Flair lying in blood before the program went to commercial.

When the program returned, the commentators appeared onscreen, explaining their horror over Jericho's "humiliating attack" on the wrestling legend. They interrupted this shocked commentary to remind the viewer that *Raw* is the longest-running show in episodic television history. At the next fight, Jeff Hardy and Dolph Zigler jumped in and out of the ring, grabbing folding chairs and steel trash cans as weapons, performing acrobatic flips on the ropes, and throwing each other around the ring. The commentators again served as narrators for the viewer, suggesting possible injuries that could result from the combat, naming some moves, and promising more action at the upcoming pay-per-view championship, *Wrestlemania*. Dolph Zigler soon emerged victorious over Jeff Hardy, and then grabbed a microphone to challenge Jeff's brother to more action at *Wrestlemania*. In comparison to the first conflict between Flair and Jericho, there was little narrative drama and a longer and more balanced display of athletic showmanship by the two wrestlers. The commentators spent little time explaining a history of animosity between the two fighters. When this fight ended, the commentators moved immediately to a more involved story line, synopsizing a romantic triangle that had developed between Paul "The Big Show" Wight, Adam "Edge" Copeland, and Vickie Guerrero. Guerrero has a long history in the WWE, appearing in fights with her late husband, Eddie Guerrero, and in subsequent feuds following his death. On this particular episode, rival wrestler John Cena provided narrative background to the viewer by reading a Get Well card to Guerrero, which allowed *Raw* producers to include footage of the previous fight between Edge and The Big Show. This event had seemingly resulted in injury to Guerrero, who had appeared with the two rivals. The live audience roared as Cena mocked Guerrero's looks and boasted about his impending win against both fighters at *Wrestlemania*. Then *Raw* broke for commercial.

When they came back from commercial, an eight-man tag-team wrestling match began. Like the Hardy–Zigler fight, commentators gave little information in this match about the fighters in the ring; instead, they discussed the upcoming *Wrestlemania* event, its dangers and potential thrills, and the financial rewards coming to its ultimate winner. *Raw* went to commercial without resolving this acrobatic fight, so it continued when the program resumed. Heavily muscled men in costumes designed to highlight their assumed identities threw one another around the ring. The match ended when all eight wrestlers came into the ring to brawl and the fans at the live event went wild, applauding and holding up versions of WWE championship belts. Just when it appeared that the match had a winner, one of the wrestlers grabbed a ladder and slammed others with it. This particular wrestler, dressed in emerald green shorts with a gold shamrock on them, was soon joined on the mat by a short, red-headed man dressed in a leprechaun costume. At this point, *Raw* again broke for commercial.

At the return, there were a series of reminders about the upcoming *Wrestlemania* event before the viewer was returned to the commentators, who opined about the terrible fight between Flair and Jericho at the start of the program. Then they moved to yet another important story line, a feud between Triple H and Randy Orton. This story line is one of the most complicated of the series, and by this episode it involved violence spilling over into the private lives of both fighters, which nevertheless had been caught by WWE cameras and could be aired for the program. After their brief recap, the action returned to the Edge–Big Show fight. Edge entered the stadium to tumultuous applause, wearing his world heavyweight championship belt while commentators explained the back story, and Guerrero, confined to a wheelchair from her injuries, was wheeled in to watch. After another commercial interruption, Edge approached Guerrero for a kiss, and when she turned her face away, the crowd cheered. Then Big Show appeared for the match and also approached Guerrero, who turned away at his attempts to approach her. In case the drama was lost on the viewers, the commentators explained that she was angry at and in love with both men, and the matter would ultimately be resolved during the upcoming match between the two men at *Wrestlemania*. Soon, John Cena again appeared on screen in the arena, chiding both wrestlers by saying, "Everyone watching at home, everyone sitting in the arena, they're laughing at you because neither of you is acting like men." Cena ended his diatribe with an insult aimed at Guerrero, and then the fighting began. As before, there was a series of acrobatic tosses and throws, punctuated by the athletes addressing Guerrero ringside. The commentators continued to explain the background feud narrative, as well as punctuate the action with explanation. As Big Show tied Edge into the ropes and prepared to attack him, Guerrero left her chair pleading with Big Show not to hurt him, and her medical attendant entered the ring to help. Soon Big Show was victorious, but he was spurned when he approached Guerrero. The match ended, but not the drama. The commentators plugged *Wrestlemania*, and *Raw* went to commercial (*Raw* 2009).

Raw delivered two more matches, recaps of past action, numerous plugs for the upcoming *Wrestlemania* event, and even a new story line before moving to the climax of the evening, the confrontation between Randy Orton and Triple H, which left the ultimate determination of champion unresolved in anticipation of *Wrestlemania*. At this point in my description, the pattern of narrative drama, sports spectacle, and self-promotion should be clear, so I will concentrate on the ethnographic context. In my experience of WWE consumption among Somali Bantu, there are observable gendered practices in the way teenagers engage with these three separate elements of WWE programming.

Teenage Engagement with WWE

As a spectacle of athleticism, Somali Bantu boys demonstrate a keen appreciation for the physical elements of wrestling as sport. In my conversations about the WWE with the teenage boys, many indicated that they liked to watch a particular wrestler for his characteristic move, not simply because of his role in a particular narrative arc. In fact, the physical display is the part of the genre that renders the discussion over whether the sport is real or fake insignificant within this group. Like Ibraahin, most of the boys indicated at some point that they knew or at least suspected that the matches were staged; likewise, most ultimately indicated that the issue was irrelevant because the wrestlers still must perform the physicality of their roles successfully within the staging. Mark Workman has noted that professional wrestling operates out of two frames that make it difficult to classify generically, staged theater drama and authentic sporting event. He argues that fans tend to fall along a continuum of interaction in which the two frames act as opposite poles (Workman 1977, 17). In my discussion with Hanad and Mahdi, the two demonstrated this sense of variable frame analysis. At the start of the match I described above, the question of whether it was an authentic sporting event came up immediately because I indicated discomfort in watching a young man, Jericho, attack and bloody an older one, Flair. As I expressed dismay that a respected elder would be beaten in such a violent way, both young men sought to alleviate my concern. Hanad helpfully pointed out to me that Flair is stronger than any of us, and therefore not to be pitied, and if he arrived in the apartment while we were viewing the fight, he could beat us all up. He cautioned me not to feel any concern about him. When I asked about the bleeding, Mahdi underscored the irrelevance of the violence onscreen and, to some extent, the central point of WWE drama by noting, "they get a lot of pay whether it's real or fake." The teenagers recognized that both men were performers, and they admired their work as such.

While the seeming violence of the sport was deemed largely irrelevant by the boys, the performance of combat was a matter of considerable interest. The boys repeatedly noted that, regardless of whether the action is real, the wrestlers are all in top physical condition, and they engage in highly athletic moves, such as flips and throws. As these particular matches played out on screen, Mahdi repeatedly pointed out to me the characteristic moves of each wrestler and expressed admiration for their performance. Likewise, Hanad, who has begun a performance dance troupe for male Somali Bantu teenagers, was also interested in the choreography demonstrated in the ring. In his writing on professional wrestling as melodrama, Henry Jenkins notes that sporting melodrama allows for the display of physical prowess within a narrative event. In the case of the WWE, that display becomes a spectacle characterized by ongoing cycles of physical vulnerability and restored potency (Jenkins 1997, 53). In her analysis of the sport, Sharon Mazer ties this spectacle specifically to the performance of masculinity, noting that "professional wrestling explicitly and implicitly makes visible cultural and countercultural ideas of masculinity and sexuality. Wrestling's apparently conservative masculine ideal is constantly undermined through the parodic, carnivalesque presentation of its opposite" (Mazer 1998, 4). Beyond the flamboyant costumes of certain characters, this carnivalesque presentation is also apparent in the performance of violence as well. In the on-going rivalry between Orton and Triple H, for example, there was a series of increasingly outrageous violent inversions of the narrative over the course of multiple episodes. What began with Orton harming members of Triple H's family moved next to an attack by Triple H on Orton's home and girlfriend, which then moved inside the arena as H imprisoned one of Orton's tag-team partners alone in the ring and attacked him with a sledgehammer. In the episode described above, Orton avenged his partner by handcuffing Triple H to the ring ropes and demanding that H's wife come and beg for his life as Orton wielded his own sledgehammer. The episode ended with H's wife prostrate and unconscious on the mat, H unable to reach her from his cuffed position on the side, and Orton stroking his sledgehammer as he moved between the two weighing his options. This model of masculinity reinforces the use of physical prowess and usually violence to achieve one's ends. At the same time, the violence is clearly performed and not real. Like a serial television program, *Raw* cuts to commercial at critical points of violence in the drama, suspending any kind of consequence to the violence. A bleeding Ric Flair is not removed by an ambulance, and Orton does not deliver the fatal blow to either H or his wife. The strongest man wins for the moment, until the next round of performed violence, in which his antagonist will have gained in strength and power.

It is perhaps not surprising that such a performance of masculinity is highly compelling to a group of young men whose lives so far have included flight from the security of home; a decade or more in massive Kenyan refugee camps where violence, particularly sexual violence against women, was a constant threat (Musse 2004; Nowrojee and Thomas 1993); and resettlement to a new country where their economic opportunities are limited by their English-language skills and lack of previous education. Mazer notes that, in professional wrestling, "victory always equals masculinity" (1998, 5). For Ibraahin, Haaruun, Hanad, Mahdi, and their male peer group, the restored potency through physical prowess offered in all WWE narratives, and its corresponding potential for providing wealth, makes not only for compelling viewing but also for a compelling vision of how to be a man. I noted previously that, when they discuss their experience of the refugee camps, most teen boys describe primarily the sense of physical danger they felt there from other groups, and many find the surrounding African American community in their housing project similarly threatening. Furthermore, these boys know that their future ability to support themselves and, eventually, a family depends on their ability to perform physical labor, as the educational system has already proved extremely difficult, and their only hopes for higher education depend on athletic skill, another type of physical labor. Consequently, the ongoing WWE narrative, in which the strongest man always wins, validates their own hopes for a secure and prosperous future for themselves through physical strength.

The second element of WWE programming, the narrative drama, is the element that is equally attractive to both teen boys and girls. The separate, complex, and largely incredible story lines acted out by the wrestlers were well known among teenagers. While I watched this episode of *Raw*, for example, all of the teenagers present provided me with deeper background on the individual rivalries than what was offered from the commentators. As part of the experience watching the program with the teenagers, for example, I learned more about Vickie Guerrero and her history on the program, and about how the feud between Orton and Triple H began, as well as the level of violence that had already been visited on their individual families. Likewise, in instances when I had discussed the WWE with the teenagers away from this instance of viewing, they often named favorite wrestling characters and described their current intrigues within the WWE narrative. Drama scholars point out that the open-ended, cyclical, and melodramatic model of narrative structure featured on the WWE, and often demonstrated in other televised sports, is one shared by daytime soap operas. Initially, this type of drama was framed as a feminine model, but as mass-mediated sporting events have increasingly adopted it, analysis has turned away from its gendered aspects and toward its overarching popularity. Melodramas, like soaps and wrestling, allow the narrative to continue past individual media encounters, remaining only temporarily resolved. Further, they allow viewers to move into an emotional register, ultimately collapsing the boundary between television screen and sporting event. The spectator becomes part of the action, calling plays and arguing with officials (Rose and Friedman 1997, 4, 9). This collapsing of the boundary between spectator and participant is particularly true of the Somali Bantu males, and will be further considered in the discussion on consumer practices later in this chapter.

In his analysis of professional wrestling specifically, Jenkins considers wrestling as popular theater staged to ensure the maximum emotional impact while directing viewers toward a specific vision of the social and moral order. Put simply, professional wrestling championships are staged as battles of higher justice where victories are granted to the virtuous (Jenkins 1997, 54–55). The reinforcement of a particular moral economy happening in WWE stories was underscored in my experience with Somali Bantu teens. In the viewing experience I described above, for example, the boys typically explained the complexities of the story line in an effort to explain which fighter should win the match. They demonstrated that, like the commentators, they expected the outcome of the match to reflect some kind of narrative justice. Haajiro, on the other hand, simply summarized past feuds and offered opinions based on issues of personal attractiveness. This gender difference was repeated outside this particular viewing instance among both teen girls and boys throughout my research. Most Somali Bantu girls could name their favorite fighters, but they demonstrated little expectation that a particular match would reflect a satisfying narrative outcome. The boys typically summarized the plots that involved their favorite wrestlers in an effort to demonstrate why their picks should ultimately win. In Workman's analysis, fans who tend to view professional wrestling through the theatrical frame typically find the drama satisfying in that the ultimate outcome proves to be a triumph of good over evil (1977, 14–15). In this instance, for example, both Hanad and Mahdi wanted Triple H to win his *Wrestlemania* match-up with Randy Orton, not because H was the better wrestler—he is actually considerably older than Orton—but because Orton had victimized H's family in beginning the rivalry, so he must correspondingly be punished. Jenkins points out that this linkage between moral authority and possession of physical strength is particularly appealing to members of the working class, because it puts power in the hands of those who perform physical labor (1997, 55). Michael Ball takes that analysis a bit further, noting that the values that are reinforced are traditional working-class values, but they are sustained and reinforced through elite interpretation, which reinforces stereotypes and feeds corporate profit (1990, 141, 157).

The feeding of corporate profit is the third element of the WWE that has proved compelling to Somali Bantu youths, who consume not just the television programming but also multiple strains of WWE product. In addition to *Raw* and *Smackdown*, teenagers also engage with the WWE on the Internet and through the purchase of consumer products. These interactions often push the world of the WWE into the unmediated lives of the boys, connecting them tangibly to the larger social imaginary that they encounter on television. To an extent, this consumer activity is ostensive, in that it allows the teenagers to enact a role within the WWE rather than simply retell a story from outside their personal experience. Ostensive patterns among adolescents have been well documented, particularly in the phenomenon of legend-tripping, where teens find a way to insert themselves into local legends—particularly those involving death and violence—by visiting the sites of these legends and interacting with the story in some way, a practice that often subsequently evolves into a localized rite of passage (Ellis [1991] 1996). In the case of these refugee boys, the purchase of WWE goods allows them to extend the television spectacle and narrative, as well as its valorization of physical prowess, into their ordinary lives. For example, early in my fieldwork, Mahdi acquired an imitation WWE championship belt. Because he lives in his grandparents' apartment at Wedgewood near other extended family, Mahdi's home is frequently filled with a large number of very young cousins and older siblings who typically display very little respect for individual personal property. The belt, however, was always treated with considerable care and respect whenever it made its way into the common space. In my visits to the home, the belt was routinely kept away from the small children, who consequently bypassed seemingly more interesting children's toys to find it for play. Even the older siblings prioritized the preservation of this particular item. In short, the family treated the belt as if Mahdi had obtained it through some kind of personal achievement, rather than simply purchased it as a consumer good. The belt, which does indeed represent achievement for fighters in the WWE, also came to represent accomplishment for Mahdi.

This representational pattern further extended into school. On the last day before winter break, as the high school that these students attend held its annual event to celebrate the diverse cultural backgrounds of their students, there was an arm-wrestling tournament for the male students. It moved through multiple rounds of play, and eventually ended as a contest between Hanad and one of his West African classmates. Although there was a variety of activities available to students, as the championship match began, most of the African male and female students gathered around to see the final outcome. Before a crush of fellow students, Hanad soundly defeated his counterpart. As the Somali Bantu students celebrated this victory, Mahdi—who had been eliminated in an earlier round—brandished his WWE belt as he escorted Hanad away from the site of the match and the clutch of fellow student spectators. The belt was a useful emblem of both Hanad's individual and the Somali Bantu students' collective athletic achievement. In addition to connecting the boys into the world of the WWE, the belt also elevated the school victory demonstrating the significance of masculine strength within their actual lived environment.

Conclusion

In his discussion on cultural reproduction in an era of dislocation, Appadurai remarks that the "pains of cultural reproduction in a disjunctive global world are, of course, not eased by the effects of mechanical art (or mass media)" because the media provides to young people "counternodes of identity," contrary to parental desires in which new gender politics and violence are included. In his opinion, the difficult task of reproducing "the family-as-microcosm of culture" is often drowned out by the loud background soundtrack playing out the fantasies of the new ethnoscape (1996, 45). However, the media consumption of these Somali Bantu teens indicates a far more complex and ambiguous relationship between the fantasies of the new ethnoscape and the reproduction of the family as a microcosm of culture, one that has clear differences along gender lines. For the Somali Bantu girls, the proliferation of African dramas allows them to explore social imaginaries that connect them to traditional gendered roles, and the viewing experience is heavily influenced by other adult community members. For the immediate present, their choices are shaped by this social imaginary, and most of the girls aim to make progress toward socially sanctioned goals of marriage and the acquisition of their own households and its traditional roles. It remains to be seen, however, how the work of cultural reproduction will continue as they begin to raise a new generation. For the Somali Bantu boys, on the other hand, the U.S. social imaginary is far more accessible through the consumption of professional wrestling and its products. While this programming stresses the resolution of complex dramas of justice and the defense of the home through contests of physical strength, arguably reproducing traditional African warrior roles, it is through the consumption of commercially available WWE products that boys extend these dramas into their real lives, connecting U.S. symbols of achievement with their adolescent lives through participation in commerce.

The repeated acquisition of information on gender identity through media consumption, whether through instruction by female elders in the appropriate domestic role of wife, or in the performance of strength in professional wrestling, provides a new, largely gender-segregated, ritual event for these young refugees, not unlike their traditional rites of passage. As Hamid Naficy has noted of television viewing among Iranian refugees, the watching of the event becomes its own ritual genre, a repetitive action that moves them over time from the liminal space of exile to reincorporation within the larger society (1999, 538–39). In the Iranian case, reincorporation happens through the high volume of advertisement that pulls the exiles into a consumerist lifestyle emphasizing the individual over the collective, thereby incorporating them into U.S. society not through the linear process of traditional rites of passage but through "a conflictual and dialectical process involving resistances, differences, reversals, and leaps forward during which features of both liminality and incorporation may coexist for quite some time" (1999, 563). For both teen boys and girls within this community, it is too soon to know whether traditional gender roles will be reproduced or reinvented by the long-term dialectical process of adolescence in America. However, it is clear that their media consumption is an important, emerging element in the construction of social identity as men and women.

Attaining Adulthood 2

Adolescence, Identity, and FGC in Diaspora

*T*he preceding chapter ended by noting the uncertainty around the process of adolescence and how it would affect the reproduction of traditional gender roles within the Somali Bantu community. While a rites-of-passage approach to the life cycle may be the dominant one among Somali Bantu adults, it is not the only model of becoming an adult available to these teenage refugees. At this point, it is time to consider the model of attaining adulthood that is most familiar to the teachers and resettlement professionals who are guiding Somali Bantu families through the early stages of integration into the United States: adolescence. This chapter will begin with an overview of literature on adolescence, with an emphasis on ethnographic research that has been conducted among adolescents. Then, since it is such a crucial concept in understanding cultural, gender, and life cycle affiliation, it will explore the notion of identity as it is understood in folkloristics.

Processes of Identity Development

Despite Bourdieu's attempt to analyze rites of passage as a universal human practice, much of the theorizing on initiation ritual has resulted from ethnographic study of communities removed from modernity. Meanwhile, the dominant approach to achieving adulthood in modern life is adolescence, a model of human development that features an extended period of liminality for young people, rather than a discreet ritual event. While adolescence, the period of time between childhood and adulthood characterized by the onset of puberty, is commonly viewed in the United States as a standard element in human development, the idea of it is relatively new. The first comprehensive study of adolescence was a two-volume work by G. S. Hall (1904), who introduced and defined the characteristics of adolescence for future students of psychology, using all the resources available to nineteenth-century social science. For describing the seeming universality of this turbulent period in the human life cycle, the work was groundbreaking and became canonical in the scholarship of human development almost immediately. Published as it was in early twentieth-century America, Hall's book coincided with late nineteenth-century labor and educational reforms in the United States designed to remove young people from the workforce and require them to remain in school later in their development. Some argue that the work is directly tied to this historic context and filled a need to introduce adolescence to scholars of human development, a purpose that undercuts its own central claim of the universality of this phase in the life course. Nevertheless, Hall's work, with its chapters on psychological and physiological fundamentals in adolescence, remained definitive for many scholars well into the early twentieth century, and a standard bearer for those who define the period as biological.

The first scholar to take notable exception to Hall's master work was the anthropologist Margaret Mead, whose ethnographic study of human development in Samoa took direct aim at the universalist claims by Hall and other psychologists. Mead argued not only that the model of adolescence present in U.S. society was a cultural construction but, more specifically, that the storm and stress that Hall defined as characteristic of all adolescence is actually a symptom of the complexity of choices facing American teenagers. Mead argued that the vast array of choices, and the resulting stresses they placed on young people, were not evident in Samoa, where educational processes were essentially reproductive of society. As a result, the transition from childhood to adulthood was, according to Mead's research, smooth and of limited duration ([1928] 1961).

In the period following these two seminal works, a number of scholars have participated in the debate over whether adolescence is a biological universal or socially constructed. In fact, this debate mirrors a similar discussion about another space on the human life cycle: childhood. In his highly influential work, Ariès argued that childhood itself was an invention of modernity rather than a universal human experience throughout time (1962). Ariès based his argument on artistic renderings of and contemporary references to children throughout the late medieval and early modern period. Of course, his claim has been the subject of lively scholarly debate, as has the question of adolescence. In general, this debate tends to break down along disciplinary categories, with psychologists (and by extension the medical and hard sciences) making universal claims about both the existence and characteristics of adolescence (Clair, Karp, and

Yoels 1993; Kett 1977; Kiell 1964), while anthropologists (and by extension most social scientists) argue that this period in the life cycle is culturally constructed (Bakan [1971] 1972; Muuss, Velder, and Porton [1975] 1996; Thorne 1993). However, an influential work coauthored by an anthropologist and a psychologist claims the universality of adolescence by combining research approaches. Schlegel and Barry (1991) attempt to prove their claim based on a vast array of anthropological literature, most of it from premodern societies. In their book, they create a catalog of ethnographic studies to support their argument about universality, but in doing so, the ethnographic details of these studies are submerged into grand overarching trends (not unlike van Gennep's work) and become less and less distinctive.

It is not my purpose here to claim one approach to the life course over another; rather, it is to contrast two different approaches held by the adults who influence the lives of the Somali Bantu teens I observed trying to navigate a variety of expectations. Regardless of whether it is a universal part of human development, adolescence is the central practice of most Western groups, including school systems in the U.S. Midwest. Consequently, it is worth considering how the practice of it has been analyzed among ethnographers. There have been a number of distinctive ethnographic studies of the teen years in a modernist context conducted by both sociologists and anthropologists. Significantly, in a number of these studies, a central element that reappears over time is the way U.S. adolescents create a rite of passage through specific activities, such as college fraternity initiations (Leemon 1972), or sexual and intellectual development in college generally (Moffatt 1989). Further, uniquely adolescent practices have been taken up by a number of popular writers who have focused on adolescent rites of passage, particularly among at-risk groups. Many of these works discuss strategies for incorporating seemingly traditional rites of passage into various social service programs (Mahdi, Christopher, and Meade 1996; Mahdi, Foster, and Little 1987), while other popular works provide accounts of the formation of individual identity, whether as adolescents in the United States (Frosch 1994) or within a variety of culture groups (Adiele and Frosch 2007). It seems that, even amid the prevailing model of extended liminality, many analysts see some value to a specific ritual passage from one role to the other.

Increasingly, there are more complex approaches to teens emerging from the ethnographic literature. In recent studies, anthropologists have concentrated on identity construction particularly among minority or migrant students, whether by focusing on how the school system creates national citizens for Hispanic kids in Texas (Foley 1990) or second-generation Sikhs in Britain (K. Hall 2002). In addition, under the influence of globalization and migration theorists

(Appadurai 1996; Hannerz 1989), youth culture has become an increasingly popular topic for anthropologists, and adolescents are increasingly being studied as agents in the creation of their own symbols and meanings within diasporic culture, itself a circumstance of extended liminality. As a result, a number of essay collections have been published with case studies of the emerging expressive culture of largely diasporic youth and its resulting commoditization (Amit-Talai and Wulff 1995; Maira and Soep 2005; Nilan and Feixa 2006). With the increased attention on youth and their choices, the field of knowledge about them is growing swiftly.

Yet a question remains that seems equally germane to understanding both the Somali Bantu youth in this study as well as the larger surrounding youth culture within which they interact. That question is about finding the ultimate destination: adulthood. Social psychologist James E. Coté has noted that the twentieth century produced changes to the Western life cycle that allowed for a prolonged adolescence, one in which individuals self-direct their own maturation in contrast to adulthood being conferred by a community ritual. Yet the individual is not left entirely to himself, as Coté observes that as the structures of the community have diminished in significance, the influence of consumer culture has grown (Coté 2000, 27–33). I noted in the introduction that Somali Bantu teens are navigating turbulent waters as both the ethnic identity and practices surrounding rites of passage are in flux. In chapter 3, I discussed the influence of consumer culture on boys as they learn about gender roles. For the moment, it is important to recognize that all teens are navigating a passage into adulthood that is influenced by social authorities, including the media and surrounding consumer culture, and that the teens who made up this study are navigating—and finding ways to integrate—two very different understandings of their place within the life cycle, both a traditional one that comes with expectations from the community authorities, and also a modernist one that imposes expectations on them through school and daily life in the United States.

Rites, Passages, Identity, and Folklore

Since the aim of this study is to explore what social and cultural tools young refugees grasp to navigate the turbulent waters of identity construction when they have a variety of cultural practices to choose from, and ethnic, gender, and age course roles are in flux, I want to take a moment to explore the notion of identity. So far, I have discussed this idea as if it is a construct universally understood by scholars across multiple academic disciplines and chronological time. It has often been used in such a way, without problematizing its meaning within different analytical contexts. Increasingly, however, identity has become the subject of considerable academic discussion, particularly among folklorists, because of its centrality to the discipline. Although he never used the word, a number of scholars have pointed out that Johann Gottfried Herder's idea, that the soul of a people could be found in its folksongs, articulates the notion of cultural identity in the language of eighteenth-century scholarship (Abrahams 2003; Dundes 1989; Oring 1994). In Herder's understanding, identity was intimately tied into the land-language-lore equation, which identified folk groups by their discrete and presumably isolated communities where they shared a body of expressive culture that could be used to characterize, or identify, them. While the discipline has evolved over the centuries, Elliot Oring notes that its driving concern has always been how the expressive culture of a group revealed something deeper about its character (1994, 223), some kind of cultural essence, what many now understand as identity. Further, Roger Abrahams notes, folklorists have generally naturalized identity into a universal element of all culture groups throughout the discipline's history (2003, 205). This essence has been a fundamental element of folkloristic inquiry from its inception.

In the larger academic world, the notion of identity as a fundamental concept of human experience began to circulate largely through the work of psychologist Erik Erikson, whose 1959 work *Identity and the Life Cycle* ultimately spawned cross-disciplinary interest in identity formation despite its original focus on individual human development. Erikson theorized that ego formation begins in individuals as infants attempt to overcome obstacles in the way of their desires for food and comfort. As individuals grow, their struggles to overcome obstacles and meet their own desires in a culturally appropriate way advance them through stages of personal growth. As an individual advances through these stages, he develops a sense of continuity as an individual over time and in varying social situations. This sense of continuity is what Erikson described as ego identity. Although Erikson theorized about individual identity development, he noted that the sociocultural surroundings provide guidance and support to lessen the trauma and stress of development, often providing a space that allows for exploration within a developmental stage, such as school or a liminal space, which he called a psychosocial moratorium. Particularly noteworthy for the community in this study, Erikson (1959) further described what obstructs the process of development. If an obstacle is too advanced or prolonged, or lacks meaning, the individual experiences identity crisis, a damaging phenomenon he encountered in his experience working with shell-shocked solders in World War II. Likewise, without the occasional moratorium, or with little sociocultural guidance, the individual can become lost. It is striking that, at this time of crisis both in the cultural history of the Somali Bantu community and individual development of its adolescents, initiation ritual—a central means for the community to provide sociocultural guidance during the development of its youth—is under particular strain.

By the 1960s Erikson's ideas had created new discourses on identity in a number of different disciplines. Among students of culture, *identity* increasingly came to be understood as the sense of continuity over time that defines a particular group, rather than simply the individual, as in Erikson's writing. In other words, Herder's soul of a people gained a new name; however, it is still represented fundamentally through the group's expressive culture. Folklorist Alan Dundes tied the two together in his highly influential definition of the folk group as "any group of people whatsoever who share at least one common factor," noting that members of the group know the common core of traditions that provide the group with identity (1989, 11). Further, Dundes notes that group identity depends on common traditions, customs, and genres of folklore: "It is important to recognize that folklore is not simply a way of obtaining available data about identity for social scientists. It is actually one of the principal means by which an individual and a group discovers or establishes his or its identity" (1989, 35). In other words, it is through the practice of expressive culture that group identity is constructed, whether that group is based on gender, ethnicity, status within the life cycle, or any other number of elements.

This understanding is particularly critical in a group of people, such as the Somali Bantu, who are developing an identity out of a number of related but disparate groups. As this group identity expands as a container of meaning, members of the group are faced with different contexts—Somali villages, Kenyan refugee camps, American housing projects—in which to practice the common core of traditions that construct and perpetuate identity. This project does not aim to catalog these in any comprehensive manner, but to examine teenagers in a particular context to understand how identity develops in the midst of dislocation and disruption. Helpful in this instance is Richard Bauman's caution against the assumption that folklore is esoteric, created within the group and held consistently over time, in which tradition bearers "carry the folklore traditions on through time and space like so much baggage" (1971, 32–33). Rather, he argued that some folklore gets created as differential identity, an idea that resonates with Erikson's idea that identity develops through the overcoming of obstacles; it does not naturally emerge without some outside stimulus. Bauman suggested that identity is constructed to differentiate group members from outsiders, an idea that correlates with Bourdieu's note above about the role of rites of passage in particular.

In fact, among the variety of folkloristic genres available to any community for establishing identity, I contend that initiation ritual is the practice that is most self-consciously aimed at constructing identity within a culture group. For the individual, the liminal period of initiation provides an Eriksonian psycho-social moratorium, a space that allows for exploration within a developmental stage. For the community, it provides a forum to establish and reaffirm group identity, a conspicuous model for the Dundesian argument about the use of folklore in identity construction. Barbara Myerhoff points out that, in fact, the rites of passage are characterized largely by paradox, integrating culture with biological destiny, celebrating change while reinforcing cultural continuity, and affecting individuals while reinforcing their identity within a community of meaning (1982, 109–11). The individual and the communal are intimately tied together. In them, regardless of the specifics of the ritual, its practice remains critical for both the individual and the community to define itself.

The Role of Individuality

In fact, the extent to which an individual chooses her participation in cultural identity is a significant question among scholars. In his work on ethnicity, for example, Fredrik Barth shifted from the Herderian equation in which race equals culture equals language, and argued that individuals use ethnic identities to categorize themselves. What appears as cultural similarities are actually elements that the individual actors see as significant. Some features are emblems of difference from other groups, for example, while others are ignored. Ultimately, while cultural content may be exhibited by overt features like dress, language, house form, and so forth, having an ethnic identity "implies a claim to be judged, and to judge oneself, by those standards that are relevant to that identity" (Barth 1969, 13–14). So, within an ethnic identity, there is a range of circumstances in which identity can be successfully realized, but there are also limits, or boundaries, that are excluded. In this understanding, an ethnic identity persists through a limited set of cultural features that differentiate the group from other groups, according to the choices of individuals (38). In contrast, Abrahams points out that the role of the individual in the adoption of cultural identity differs depending on historical and geographic circumstances. Specifically, in areas of ethnic conflict, he notes, "identity formation is not optional.

You are what you are born into or what you are designated to be by the state or dominant group" (Abrahams 2003, 207). On the American side of the Atlantic, he argues, "identity lies at the heart of how each of us may find a way to confront the equally slippery concepts of individuality and community" (208). In other words, in the United States, identity is a Barthian choice made by individuals with alternatives, a marked contrast to the sense of identity as inherited by birth and reinforced through initiation ritual common in southern Somalia.

This distinction suggests a critical perspective for this research project. These young people have been born into a model of identity based on their birth within a culture group, and continued participation in that group has traditionally been reinforced by initiation ritual. Now they find themselves exposed to a system of identity choices in the midst of flight on one continent and resettlement on another. Abrahams argues that this age of increasing migration and diaspora will eventually scuttle the concept of identity, noting: "Identity will simply not hold up as a container of meaning under the conditions of the postindustrial world in which people move or are moved at a moment's notice" (2003, 217). However, his insight contrasts strikingly with that of Stuart Hall, who noted two different ways of thinking about cultural identity, particularly for those in diasporic communities. The first implies a notion of shared culture hiding within individuals that "reflects the common historical experiences and shared cultural codes which provide us, as 'one people,' with stable, unchanging, and continuous frames of reference and meaning beneath the shifting divisions and vicissitudes of our actual history" (2003, 234), a particularly powerful idea in the midst of dislocation. It is also one that underscores the significance of initiation ritual, particularly one that inscribes identity through modification of the physical body because, for the various groups that compose the Somali Bantu culture group, it is a cultural process that provides continuity over time. Hall's second notion, however, recognizes that shared history is full of ruptures and discontinuities, and identity is always in the process of becoming; it is the name "we give to the different ways we are positioned by, and position ourselves within, the narratives of the past" (2003, 236). So identity can be shaped by rupture and struggle, but it may also be supplanted by these two elements as well. Given the seeming importance of ritual practice within the Somali Bantu community historically, and the experience of rupture and discontinuity that has been a consistent part of the lives of these teenage refugees, these complex questions about the construction and transmission of identity within it are not merely academic but also resonate in the decisions they and their families and teachers make within their daily and ritual lives. Consequently, I will take up the question of what appears to be happening ritually among this community as a result of displacement from southern Somalia and resettlement to North America.

Genital Cutting in Diaspora

So far, this chapter has concentrated on research and analysis of adolescence in the ethnographic literature and identity construction within culture groups overall. At this point, it is time to turn back to the teens who are the focus of this study to briefly note what is known about the practice of genital cutting among Somalis in diaspora, how U.S. legal authorities are reacting to genital cutting with the arrival of significant East African groups, and what can therefore be inferred about the refugee teens whose stories appear within these pages.

While most analysts of FGC note the difficulty in obtaining data on the prevalence of the various practices (Shell-Duncan and Hernlund 2000, 7–9; World Health Organization 2008, 23, 25), international statistics derived from numbers collected at the national level note that the practice of female genital cutting in Somalia was at 97.9 percent in 2005 (World Health Organization 2008, 6). Likewise, working from figures supplied by the World Bank and United Nations Population Fund in 2004, Gele et al. characterize Somalia as having the highest rate of FGC prevalence in the world, at 99 percent (Gele et al. 2012). For female initiates in Somalia, genital cutting involves infibulation. Although there is limited quantitative data available about the continued practice of genital cutting in refugee camps or in resettlement, the ubiquity of the practice in contemporary Somalia, and among members of the Somali Bantu community historically, suggest that it remained widespread among the Somali Bantu in diaspora at least until resettlement to the United States began in 2003–4.

Despite the lack of quantitative information available on diasporic practice, there appear to be some discernable trends emerging. Based on studies of ethnic Somalis in diaspora, it would seem that resettlement is displacing the notion that identity rests in the practice of genital cutting. Both Berns-McGown and Johnsdotter have noted that, in exile, the significance of Islamic religious identity has grown. One outcome of this shift has been an increased questioning of cultural practices that are not directly tied to Islam, which includes FGC. As a result, there is a trend among ethnic Somalis in London, Toronto, and Sweden toward *sunna* practices that do not result in a long-term alteration of girls' genitalia, such as pricking the clitoris (Berns-McGown 1999; Johnsdotter 2007). Johansen further observes that, in Norway, the enclosure mentality among diasporic Somalis is moving from infibulation to veiling. Not only has veiling become more of a standard before marriage in the diasporic context than it was in East Africa, where it typically occurred at marriage, but as a phenomenon, it also increases in contexts where Somali women are exposed to the Norwegian public in mixed arenas, but decreases in African-dominated contexts (Johansen 2007, 260–61). Beyond the connection with Muslim identity, it appears that FGC practices in diaspora are still shaped by the question of marriageability. Johansen notes that ethnic Somalis resettled in Norway are exposed—and often educated—in a system with a Norwegian view of the natural body. As a result, the sexual expectations of both genders are changing. If ethnic Somali men who are raised in Norway increasingly perceive an uninfibulated female body as natural and, significantly, more desirable, then being infibulated will have a negative impact on the prospect of marriageability for girls within the community. As a result, diasporic Somalis in Sweden see that infibulation could increasingly become an impediment to marriage rather than necessary to it, as it would have been in Somalia, so there has been a reconsideration of requiring it for their girls (113). The social anthropologist Aud Talle cautions about seeing this trend as completely positive, arguing that while diasporic Somalis have become much more forthright in their condemnation of the practice, there are negative consequences to such a swift and significant cultural shift. She points out that something that had been considered beautiful has now become ugly, a mark of decreased worth inscribed on the bodies of Somali women, marking them as incomplete and inferior, or mutilated humans in "a story they have not written themselves; in fact, their bodies have become sites of a worldwide discourse on morality" (Talle 2007, 103). Likewise, as noted by Ahmadu (2000, 2007) and Declich (1995a, 1995b) in chapter 2, FGC also reinforces matriarchal power, and shifts in ritual practice that disempower female authority figures specifically can disempower women generally.

Nevertheless, dislocation and resettlement has resulted in changing perceptions within the greater Somali community. At this stage in the resettlement of the Somali Bantu to the United States, however, I am unaware of any conclusive research about FGC practices that would demonstrate whether resettlement has affected genital modification for either boys or girls. My interviews with resettlement staff and medical professionals assigned to the community in the early period of the resettlement indicates that many refugee children (generally from age four or older) undergo the cutting aspects of the ritual in the East African camps before coming to the United States, which corresponds to Gele and colleagues' (2012) observation that FGC is usually performed in Somalia on children before the age of nine. Presumably, these attempts to keep children physically in conformity with tradition and their parents in conformity with U.S. law would apply to the peer group I studied, who had all moved to the United States just before puberty.

Undoubtedly, another trend in the practice of FGC in diaspora relates to the role of the state in preventing groups from practicing it, and punishing transgressors, in the new context. In the United States, there have been a few significant legal cases that have garnered considerable public attention as increasing populations of East Africans settle here. In their work, Kratz and Piot critique two problematic asylum cases in which the asylum seeker sought refuge in the United States based on her culture group's practice of FGC. In both the cases of Fauziya Kasinga of Togo and Adelaide Abankwah of Ghana, the courts relied on claims that culture is a monolithic beast that forces African victims to do things without making an effort to seek definitive information about the practices of African culture groups in reality (Kratz 2007; Piot 2007). While the establishment of legal precedents based on African stereotypes and an unsophisticated understanding of culture as fixed and oppressive within the asylum system is problematic, the claims made on behalf of culture within the U.S. criminal justice system are even more troubling. In his book on the trial of Khalid Misri Adem, an Ethiopian man accused of removing the clitoris of his two-year-old daughter with scissors, Charles G. Steffen (2011) raises concerns about the circulating notion of culture as definitive evidence of motive for a crime. This criminal case against the immigrant grew out of a bitter custody battle but provided no forensic evidence to implicate the father rather than the mother or any other adult with means and motive in the cutting of the little girl. However, the court admitted cultural information on the practice of FGC in Ethiopia without interrogating the role culture plays in the decision-making of individuals, its complex role in the home country, or its changeable nature, particularly in diaspora. In other words, because FGC is practiced in some parts of Ethiopia, it became reasonable to assume that Adem would practice it here. His culture made him do it. As a result, Adem first lost custody of his daughter, and still remains in jail.

In coming decades, as judicial and medical structures in countries of resettlement grapple with a growing migration from Africa, they will have to examine with greater sophistication the argument that culture makes individuals do things, particularly if those things are considered child abuse. In the meantime, Hernlund and Shell-Duncan note that global migration affects not just legal and medical systems but also the most intimate decisions of family life. When traditional practices affecting women are displaced, the result is "a generation of families on the move [who] find themselves involved in a 'social experiment,' especially regarding the raising of their daughters" (Hernlund and Shell-Duncan 2007, 6).

Given that Somali Bantu refugees who were part of my study demonstrated a high level of concern about the consequence of claims of child abuse generally, and a high level of awareness that rituals of genital cutting of girls are illegal in the United States more specifically, I did not routinely question members of the community about the practice of the ritual in the United States. It seemed to me that the subject of genital cutting itself would best be left to subsequent research efforts with the community later in their resettlement experience, rather than as an initial research project while the community adjusted to landing in the United States after years in refugee camps. However, there is no question that the practice of the ritual is central to identity construction for both the culture group and the enculturated individuals. Furthermore, regardless of what is happening physically, what is clear is that the ritual context has been radically altered by dislocation and resettlement. It should also be clear at this point that initiation ritual is more than genital cutting, and much of the identity formation that previously occurred within the ritual context has been wholly disrupted, whether or not the cutting aspects of the ritual are performed. In chapter 7, I consider the significance Somali Bantu rites of passage may have as the community attempts to inculcate gender, ethnic, and life cycle identity over time.

Meanwhile, the placement of these teens into the American school system has transplanted them to a context where the model of progress toward adulthood is not a single ritual event but a totally new stage in the life cycle: adolescence. In the next chapter, we will consider the interplay between these teens and the school system as they prepare themselves for adulthood.

5

No Ritual Left Behind

Schools and American Rites of Passage

The Municipal Schools offer two levels of English as a Second Language (ESL) support to newly arrived teenage refugees. The first level is for students who have limited proficiency in English and who, like the Somali Bantu, often have no experience in formalized education, but who would not be an appropriate fit in a primary school. These students are assigned to a welcome center, a specialized school where there is a higher density of ESL resources available, and a large population of students with similar language skills in English. In a welcome center, students can start at the beginning of the educational spectrum and learn among peers in sheltered classrooms. For those students who arrive with or eventually obtain greater proficiency in English, there are also specific mainstream schools within the district where they can pursue a normal curriculum with American-born high school–aged kids and receive additional support from the ESL staff working at these designated mainstream schools. At the start of my research, I based myself at the McGuffey Welcome Center, where a significant population of Somali Bantu teenage refugees attended school. At the time, this facility was one of two centers offering a high school curriculum within the district and, because it was across town from their housing projects, most Somali Bantu students were bused to McGuffey for its ESL resources.

The program operated out of an older high school building in a lower-income neighborhood just north of the campus of a large university, and it shared the facility with the Municipal Alternative High School (MAHS), the district's magnet school for academic high achievers. The two schools, housed within the same imposing early twentieth-century structure, operated as if on two different planes of reality. Although the welcome center had its offices at the front of the building, the rest of that wing housed the classrooms and offices of MAHS. A set of double doors separated that area of the building from the Welcome Center, which was spread over two floors in a more recent wing at the back of the same school building, along with the shared cafeteria and gymnasium. While this layout meant that students from either facility would, at some time or another, need access to the wing used by the other school, the two sets of students had virtually no interactions with each other. Large signs warned them out of each other's zones, and instances of student contact were very rare. At the front of the building a high school served the needs of bright, highly motivated, college-bound American kids preparing "to be contributing citizens of the global community" (CAHS n.d.), while in the back corridor a mix of African refugees in colorful ethnic clothing, Latino migrants, and a few Asian teens—all with comparatively deeper and less encouraging experiences of that global community—prepared for life in the United States with limits both in English skills and experience with formal schooling in the United States.

After my first year of fieldwork, the district allocated the vacant Linmoor Junior High School nearby for the use of the district ESL programs, so the two high school welcome centers were merged into one school, which was renamed simply the High School Welcome Center. In an effort to maintain clarity about these separate facilities, I will refer to the two campuses by their original names, McGuffey and Linmoor, when it is necessary to distinguish between the two different parts of my field experience. When referring to the ESL program as a whole, I will use the district's designation of High School Welcome Center. The move to Linmoor proved to be significant in a number of ways. First, the ESL students occupied their own extensive school building for the first time, and it was well equipped with an auditorium, gymnasium, cafeteria, and additional classroom space. The move also consolidated the ESL resources of the district into one location, allowing for greater administrative supervision of students and district employees, and for multilingual support personnel to be located with the high school population. The move was very well received by students and staff because it gave the school a sense of permanence, offering them ownership over an academic location after many years of being marginalized within other school buildings.

In fact, on many levels, both facilities provide the experience of a mainstream high school environment: bells ring at intervals, hallways crowd, teenagers laugh and gossip, they argue and fight, then they disperse into classrooms, cafeterias, and gymnasiums; likewise, schoolwork hangs on cinder block walls, and teachers seek to maintain order in a space where they are vastly outnumbered by energetic youngsters. Regardless of the cultural background of the students within it, there is an inevitable pattern to an American high school, an everyday practice of rituals and routines that serves to structure educational life at the secondary level. At the High School Welcome Center, a sense of all-American high school normalcy is mitigated somewhat by the sounds and appearance of these students, who come from thirty different countries and speak more than twenty different languages (CCS n.d.). The ethnic Somali girls appear in monochromatic veils and dresses that cover most of their skin, while many of their Latino counterparts sport low-slung jeans and short skirts. Some of the gossip is in languages that have yet to be documented by linguists, and female ululations sometimes accompany the sounds of dismissal bells. Regardless of these unique attributes, however, the High School Welcome Center is not exempt from one overarching element of the U.S. educational system that forces conformity onto all schools nationwide: the testing regime mandated by the No Child Left Behind Act (Public Law, 107–10).

Signed into law in early 2002 by President George W. Bush, the No Child Left Behind Act (NCLB) established standards-based education reform across the nation, requiring all states that receive federal funding for schools to implement assessments in basic skills for all students at certain points in their education. What has made NCLB controversial is that future funding is tied to the test results, so ongoing student failure on the test can lead to the withdrawal of funding from the school and the district, as students move to private and charter schools, taking their financial allowance with them. Under NCLB, each state is free to set its own testing standards, as long as the students are tested in reading and mathematics. Since 2007 this state has met this testing requirement through the State Graduation Test (SGT), which has five component tests of reading, writing, math, science, and social studies. All high school students in the state take the test in the spring semester of the tenth grade and, if an individual fails it, he or she has multiple opportunities to retake the test before completing twelfth grade. Students with lower proficiency in English are given no exemption to this testing requirement under NCLB, so they are required to take the SGT as tenth-grade students. However, because the test is offered in English only, these students are allowed a longer time frame to complete each section of the test. Because ESL students are largely unsuccessful at the test, what this means in practice is that English-language learners have the potential to bring down scores districtwide. In fact, Menken details how ESL students are encouraged to drop out of their school or pursue an alternative diploma so that the school is not burdened with a lower overall score as a result of the ESL population (Menken 2008, 117). In a program like the High School Welcome Center, where these students are clustered together instead of being mainstreamed into a native English-speaking population, there is a high likelihood that the school will eventually face punitive action because their changing population of newcomers will never meet the local, state, or national standard (Custodio 2009, 8).

As a result, for administrators, teachers, and students alike, the SGT acts as a shared, central hurdle to be scaled, a quantifiable indication of district/classroom/student success. In this and many other ways, the test shares a number of significant characteristics with traditional rites of passage into adulthood. For example, passage through it has become the definitive measure of student readiness for the adult world. It has become the subject of significant anxiety as students and teachers progress toward it within the school system. Teacher effort is increasingly directed toward guiding the students through it instead of being concentrated on everyday learning. Finally, the test is conducted as a time set apart within the school, a liminal space in which normal community rules and activities are suspended while segregated initiates attempt a successful passage through it. Beyond the content material it addresses, and the immediate ritual performance, this particular rite of passage caps a deeply American and radically new way of constructing the life course for Somali Bantu teenagers, one that they absorb only slowly and manifest in subtle ways, but which defines identity over time. I would suggest that one of the most significant outcomes of participation in the American educational system for Somali Bantu students is not mastery of the content material; rather, it is the shift from a system of identity formation based solely on collective age group, gender, and ethnic affiliation to one that includes room for identity based on individual achievement.

From Collective Dependency to Individual Achievement

Early in my visits to McGuffey Welcome Center, a frustrated Rachel Morgan scolded her students in U.S. Citizenship class about their learning practices. She attempted to explain that copying homework from a friend, or copying notes instead of listening in class, is a bad thing. Using simple English to make her point, Mrs. Morgan explained, "Borrowing is cheating. You need to learn to do things on your own." She received a roomful of blank stares in response. Some weeks later, she gave a test to this same class, which was about 50 percent full of Somali Bantu teenagers. After she passed out the test, the rumble of voices grew louder rather than quieter. Students talked openly to one another seeking help and, as I walked around the room in a futile effort to scare them into silence, they begged me to supply them with answers to the test questions. Mahdi, a young man previously eager to help me understand his ethnic history and culture, tried a sympathy gambit. "Miss," he pleaded, "I'll fail if you don't just tell me what the answer is." His classmates encouraged his approach, making it clear that any "help" he received from me would be immediately shared with his friends and then widened out to a larger circle of peers. My efforts to coax him into trying on his own instead of passively receiving my help was met with a look of surprise, confusion, and sheer betrayal. At this point in our relationship, Mahdi had already painstakingly explained to me the physiological differences between Somali Bantu and ethnic Somali individuals, as well as the role of dance in Eid al-Fitr celebrations at his home, so it seemed inconceivable that I would expect him to draw lines from sixteenth-century Spanish conquistadors in one column to their corresponding American settlements in the other all by himself. As I moved through the rows of desks, students broke their own chatter only to request an answer from me. Few made an effort to actually read and complete the test. Finally, after perhaps twenty minutes of this, Mrs. Morgan had enough and collected the test, proclaiming that she would probably fail everyone on it.

Later in the class period, as students watched a film on Lewis, Clark, and Sacagawea's expedition to the Pacific, Mrs. Morgan quietly graded homework assignments from earlier in the week. Sitting near her desk, a young Somali Bantu girl named Haajiro watched the grading intently. As Mrs. Morgan put a grade on each page, Haajiro would stand up from her chair, peer at the student's name and grade, and then announce the bad news about the individual's work to the entire class. Slowly, the attention of the classroom was drawn away from the film and toward Haajiro, who was making no effort to hide her activities. In fact, she was gleefully calling out the bad news, which was met with giggles from her peers. At first, Mrs. Morgan attempted to ignore Haajiro, whom she perceived as simply immature, and kept redirecting classroom attention to the film and a large map of the United States where students could trace the explorers' routes to the ocean, to point out potential future test questions about the expedition. All of this had increasingly limited effectiveness. After Haajiro revealed many more grades, Mrs. Morgan finally lost her patience and ordered the student into a more distant seat. Before class ended, Mrs. Morgan addressed the room. "Most students have failed this assignment. You have to read the questions and find the answers in your books," she counseled. "If you are going to copy from your fellow students, you should try not to copy wrong answers— I can tell who are sharing answers because you are getting the same wrong answers. Even if you get the answer right, if you copy it off somebody else's work, it's wrong." At this news, the students erupted in uncharacteristic anger, frustrated and upset that their attempt at the assignment has not yielded them any gain, and demanding better grades just for trying. In a show of class unity despite clear ethnic cliques, they threw the assignments into the trash as the class ended to demonstrate the illegitimacy of the educational experience. "How are they ever going to learn anything?" Mrs. Morgan asked me in exasperation after this classroom meltdown. "They don't know how to work."

I begin, somewhat reluctantly, with this example of classroom frustration and failure not because it is an example of any one individual doing any particular thing wrong but because I believe it is a clear example of cultural dissonance between U.S. expectations of student participation in school and Somali Bantu expectations of work and accomplishment, and the high level of frustration such dissonance engenders on both ends of the teacher/student spectrum. While instructors certified as Teachers of English as a Second Language (TESOL), such as Mrs. Morgan, take coursework to prepare them for cultural differences—like sensitivity to eating in front of their fasting students during Ramadan or overlooking the most elaborate head coverings of the female students from Somalia—the most frustrating cultural misunderstandings typically happen over less obvious issues, where the cultural values are so deeply held that they are unstated by both parties. Habermas argues that for communication to happen effectively, there must be a shared set of implicit knowledge that goes so deep that it is typically outside of communicative action. He refers to this shared set of knowledge as a lifeworld (Habermas 1984, 337). In this case, the dissonance between Mrs. Morgan and her students demonstrates the lack of a shared lifeworld between the teacher and students. There needs to be a shared understanding of the notion of work, but in the classroom, there is only cultural difference. Mrs. Morgan, like most American teachers, expects her students to work for individual mastery of a subject, and ultimately individual progress toward achievement. Her Somali Bantu students, by contrast, understand work to be a group effort that results in success for all, regardless of one individual's contribution.

This idea of rewarding individual achievement is a deeply held cultural value in the United States, part of what Taylor describes as the modern moral order. In this order, the individual is primary, and society is constructed to preserve individual security and foster exchange and prosperity, rather than the individual serving as part of a hierarchical social structure (Taylor 2004, 19–21). This modernist moral order echoes deeply within American systems of education. Teachers may design group classroom activities and even homework assignments, but ultimately, it is the individual who is rewarded for doing his homework or passing her test. Individuals are awarded diplomas and scholarships and, one hopes, jobs. At the welcome center, this value was particularly hard for Somali Bantu students to grasp, and their inability to do so was a huge initial frustration for teachers. Mrs. Morgan was not the only teacher who expressed an early sense of futility about teaching these students. In fact, the communal sense of dependency and seeming lack of effort by students was a constant frustration, and was blamed on a variety of problems that reflect the understanding and social concerns of the teachers: dependence on the U.S.

welfare system, cultural patterns that require girls to marry young, childhood trauma affecting present-day learning, and an unwillingness to accept an American future. Initially, this cultural problem seemed to threaten the entire educational progress of these teens. However, despite its depth, over the course of my sixteen-month fieldwork experience at the school, changes in class organization and student clusters had the unintended effect of gradually changing how students perceive their own identity in school, and consequently how they expected to be rewarded within an academic framework. Theorists of education have noted that schools typically combine overt pedagogy with what they describe as the "hidden curriculum," in which values and norms are transmitted tacitly through routines, social relations, teacher expectations, and ritual events (Giroux 1983; Harris 1988; McLaren 1994). Likewise, folklorists have explored how the structures and settings established by organizations make symbols and values apparent (Jones, Moore, and Snyder 1988). In this case, the organization of classes around individual skill levels and the clustering and reclustering of students based on individual achievement served to foster an alternative American sense of identity among these refugee students.

The Reorganization of Student Peer Groups

Within a few weeks of Mrs. Morgan's testing experience, and in response to teacher suggestions for a better distribution of low performing students, the welcome center reorganized their student population into classes based on student learning levels. Rather than offering multiple sections of the same core classes to all students enrolled as ninth graders—a catchall category that included all students without the necessary language skills to take the SGT—the school reorganized the students and teachers into two different learning streams: lab classes and standard curriculum classes. Most Somali Bantu teenagers were clustered into lab classes, specialized classes designed to concentrate on language acquisition skills for students whose English was not yet at a high school level. While the lab classes were organized around a content area, such as citizenship or science, their tests and assignments were designed to reach reading and writing goals within those subjects, not primarily to provide high school level aptitude in the content material. Once a student moved through low (designed to practice kindergarten to second-grade language skills), medium (third- and fourth-grade language skills), and high (fifth- through eighth-grade language skills) lab versions of these classes, the student would then be moved into a traditional ninth-grade class at the welcome center, where he or she would be expected to gain ninth-grade understanding of the content area, even though the material would be taught at a primary school reading level (Custodio 2009). With this new organization, once a student was sorted into a group of academic peers, he or she remained with this group for all classes every day. In this way, a peer group was formed, one that stayed together in different classrooms learning different academic topics.

The unintended consequence of this administrative change was that it dismantled and restructured previous long-term classroom peer groups, an outcome that initially met with considerable confusion and, later, resistance from the students. Outside of this structure, students at the welcome center clustered in ethnic, age, and gender-based groups, both in class and in more social periods. Somali Bantu teenagers tended to sit together in classes and in the cafeteria, clustered in gender-based groups. While some of the students may have demonstrated greater proficiency in school, they tended to work in groups, sharing homework assignments and test answers, relying on more advanced students to call out correct answers in class, regardless of which student the teacher may have singled out. Within these ethnic and gender groups, there was considerable dependency on each other. Some students, like Timiro, who was a higher functioning student than her friend Maryan, would simply let Maryan copy her work rather than force her to learn the material on her own, thereby maintaining harmony within the traditional peer group. Because of such patterns, the school reorganization of students was fairly disruptive, but student resistance to it was mitigated by their increasing comfort with the level of instruction they encountered in the classroom. Rather than concentrate on which conquistadors explored which part of the Americas in the sixteenth century, students could concentrate on map skills and numbering, or sentence construction, or other achievable goals.

The reactions that came with the subsequent reorganizations were even more noteworthy. The first changes in November had been made in reaction to teacher input and came with little warning to the students. At the start of the new semester in mid-January, the school again reorganized the students based on their performance in their lab classes. At that point, a number of Somali Bantu students moved upward into intermediate and advanced lab classes, leaving only three Somali Bantu students in the low lab group. This new re-organization created greater controversy among many students, who were again unhappy with the deconstruction and reconstruction of preexisting peer groups. In this case, however, some of the discontent demonstrated that students were beginning to base their school identities on these academic labels. Many of the students who were advanced were very proud of their achievement, at least until their work level increased. Still others, like Dahabo and Haajiro, complained loudly that they belonged in even higher achieving groups; they wanted to be identified as advanced lab students, as had some of their Somali Bantu peers. What I want to emphasize is that this was the first time these students had been promoted in such a public way according to individual merit, without regard for peer groupings based on ethnicity, gender, or age. They now had labels (low intermediate, and high) based on personal achievement and for some, it was evolving into an important marker for identity.

Throughout the remainder of that academic year, a pattern emerged within this academic hierarchy. Somali Bantu students at the lower end of the achievement hierarchy, the low lab students, demonstrated very little sense of identification with their merit-based class, which was designated according to individual effort. In some instances, they chose not to participate as members of the group, opting out of class exercises and homework. They also failed to adopt the notion that individual achievement was a successful strategy for advancement. For example, upon learning that Timiro would be reassigned from the lower lab while she would not, Maryan approached school officials to ask for immediate advancement into the intermediate level, not because she could do the work, but because the person on whom she was dependent, Timiro, had been moved. The request was denied because her language skills were not sufficient to manage the intermediate material. With Timiro gone, Maryan, as the sole female Somali Bantu student left in the low lab class, tried unsuccessfully to develop new dependencies with other, non–Somali Bantu females in the class. As the semester continued, it became increasingly clear that neither Maryan nor her two male peers in the low lab class were expected to ever progress any further. Teachers tried to address their lack of progress by suggesting special education testing for all three of the students. However, at the most fundamental level, none of these three students ever demonstrated that they grasped the importance of individual achievement in the school system and, subsequently, in U.S. life. One of the male students, Maaxi, simply refused to develop his considerable leadership and speaking skills into written assignments; his classmate Haaruun refused to make any effort in homework and classroom assignments; and Maryan continued to ask others for answers rather than try to read and answer the questions herself. They never identified themselves as low learners and eschewed the demands of the school system while maintaining their indigenous systems of measuring achievement based on age group, gender, ethnic, and family ties.

On the other hand, in the intermediate class, Somali Bantu students eagerly volunteered to read aloud in class, and responded to questions asked by their teacher—even when they got it wrong. On written exercises, they moved from asking adults to supply them with answers to asking for confirmation of their attempted work. They began to understand, to borrow Mrs. Morgan's words from earlier in the year, "how to work." Among the advanced Somali Bantu students, their increasing comfort with individual achievement was even clearer. Beyond their more productive participation in classroom activities, and their deepening acceptance of the role of tests in evaluating student perform- ance, the Somali Bantu students in advanced lab classes were also beginning to anticipate a self-made future beyond the classroom. As spring approached, students in that group began to circulate ideas of what they wanted to do for a living when they finished school, something that no student had discussed with me in the early months of the school year. Likewise, when opportunities to pursue student employment began to circulate over the summer break, it was the intermediate and advanced students like Dahabo, Haajiro, and Tahlil who were most diligent about pursuing them. Maryan, on the other hand, continued to seek out a productive dependency, while Haaruun gained a reputation for leadership in the emerging Somali Bantu youth gang at Wedgewood Village Apartments.

In the autumn, the students moved to the building that had previously housed Linmoor Middle School, where the larger population of students, and the advancement of many Somali Bantu, caused even further reconfiguration of peer groups. At this point, Somali Bantu teenagers were distributed into a wider range of class sections. The ethnic clusters were still highly evident at lunch and in nonacademic programs, but no individual classes contained ex- clusively large concentrations of Somali Bantu teenagers in them. Further, the difference between students following the standard curriculum and those in lab classes became more pronounced because the two groups had separate lunch schedules. This separation within social time met with the strongest student resistance yet, and a number of welcome center students demanded that they be elevated to standard curriculum classes so that they could eat with members of their ethnic peer groups. The school administration remained firm in their new organization, however, requiring the students to pass a section of the SGT in order to advance to the standard curriculum, which prevented considerable re-sorting based on student demand.

The trends in student behavior evident after the January re-sort became even more pronounced in the fall. The students in standard classes were thrilled with their progress and new identity as fully fledged high school students. Mahdi positively gloated about his move to ninth grade despite the increased academic workload. For Mako, now in tenth grade, my visits were a chance to ask about school material, such as the Pythagorean Theorem, rather than to counsel me on how to secure a husband, as had been her fixation before school resumed that fall. Meanwhile, still in the low lab classes, Maryan informed me on my first visit of the year that "school is boring"; Haaruun laughed and shrugged his shoulders at all my attempts to communicate with him; and Maaxi had been withdrawn from school entirely, moving to another part of the country where he has family in a Somali Bantu resettlement site.

Interestingly, the greatest resistance to the fall reorganization came from the previously intermediate students. After a semester of insisting she was capable of standard classes, and a summer insisting that McGuffey was a bad school, Dahabo successfully convinced her mother to move her to West High School, a standard high school with ESL resources where she would be mainstreamed into the student population. A few weeks into the new school year, and after months of insisting they should be mainstreamed rather than stay in lab classes, siblings Haajiro and Heybe also brought their parents to school to withdraw them from the welcome center. In order to prevent the disruption of multiple transfers, the school set a new rule that students could only make such a move once during an academic year. For Heybe and Haajiro, there would be no coming back. In the following week, Ibraahin—who had already been allowed to transfer back and forth from West the previous year—also withdrew from the welcome center. In this case, the scene got very heated as school administrators tried to convince Ibraahin to stay, and an altercation broke out between the student and a Somali Bantu translator, such that Ibraahin was removed from the rolls. Mr. Vogelsong, who had invested a great deal of time and effort into Ibraahin, said sadly, "He's probably just lost his last chance at actually graduating." While this transferring trend was happening, Mahdi attempted to convince his grandparents, Abuukar and Basra, to let him move to West, but Abuukar refused, and Mahdi, who showed considerable progress in ninth-grade coursework, was ultimately glad he stayed.

Following their departures to West, there were mixed reports about the progress of these defectors from Linmoor. Ms. Hegde, a science teacher, opined that the students might actually have an easier time of it at West, because they would slip through the cracks and get passed along within the school structure of a standard high school. At a welcome center, they would get attention and would be encouraged to work harder. Mrs. Spear, the career counselor, voiced a suspicion that a number of charter schools were recruiting these students, but once they discovered how low their skills are in English, they would routinely kick them back to the public school system. With both Ibraahin and Heybe, truancy had become an issue at West and, according to Maryan, Heybe, Haajiro, and Dahabo were all struggling in their mainstream courses. But I could get little news from her about her cousin Ibraahin. "Ibraahin is stupid," she said repeatedly, indicating that he had fallen into petty thieving, even from members of the Somali Bantu community. By the end of December, Assistant Principal D'Angelo confirmed that both Ibraahin and Heybe had applied to return to the welcome center despite the contentious way they left it, but they had been refused. Late in the following spring, I visited with Heybe, Haajiro, Ibraahin, and Dahabo at West High School, and all four seemed pleased by being mainstreamed into a standard high school curriculum and claimed they were managing to maintain, if not advance, their levels of learning.

Back at the Welcome Center, the structuring of classrooms by achievement level created a daily peer group for Somali Bantu students based on academic achievement. Within these peer groups, ethnic and gender identity still remained central systems of identification and organization. However, by requiring passage through individual, performance-based tests for progress upward within this hierarchy, the school created alternate ways for Somali Bantu students to claim identity within the school system: as low, intermediate, or high language learners, or as mainstream high school students. More than the lessons they learned in citizenship class, these new achievement-based, individual identities provided an important alternative to previously immutable ethnic, gender, and age-related identities.

Intramural Soccer
and the Evolution of Identity Patterns and Maturity

This trend toward privileging individual ability over ethnic identity was not limited solely to the academic activities of the school. It was also manifest among male teenagers in sports activities at the welcome center. Because the welcome center is a special program rather than a full-service high school, the students at McGuffey and, later, Linmoor could not participate in the high school city sports leagues under any kind of school team. According to district policy, a welcome center student could be invited to join a competitive team at the high school they would attend if they did not attend the welcome center. While such participation is possible in theory, it is largely impossible in practice because the students are bused to and from the welcome center and have very limited access to private transportation. As a result, it is difficult for them to make try-outs and after-school practices at their assigned high schools, a place where they would also need to be bused. Likewise, since they do not attend those schools, they are often not well informed about opportunities to participate in extracurricular activities, like sports. As a result, none of the welcome center students played competitive sports in the public school system during my research.

However, in an effort to provide sporting events to the students, particularly the boys, and also to offer a diversion to the student body during the final two months of the school year, the McGuffey Welcome Center created a soccer tournament that played out over a series of Friday afternoons in April and May. The Arcadia Cup Tournament, named for a previous school where the welcome center had been housed, began with eight all-male teams, formed exclusively by the students. A number of the teams were created along ethnic lines. There was, for example, a team identified as exclusively Mexican, another of non-Mexican Latinos, and a team of ethnic Somalis. Most of the Somali Bantu players in the tournament had clustered onto Team Africa, a team that formed when a group of West Africans of various nationalities joined a number of Somali Bantu players. Before the union of those two African groups, some of the strongest Somali Bantu players were financially supported by Elias, an adult Palestinian student with significant financial resources for uniforms and playing fees. According to Mr. Jackson, the supervising faculty member of the tournament, Elias's deliberate team selection based on individual skill was part of a larger, long-term trend toward ethnic integration within the tournament itself. In its early years, all of the Arcadia Cup teams were ethnically affiliated, and there would be near riots from the entire ethnic group when a team lost a match. However, over time, kids who were serious about winning realized that they had a better chance with teams based less on ethnic affiliation and more on skill. With this in mind, Elias created one of the two most ethnically integrated teams in the tournament, both of which met in the championship match, with Elias's team eventually winning the cup. However, for most of the ever-changing student population, the teams garnered support based on ethnic loyalty rather than individual skill. Although the championship team included one Somali Bantu player, Ibraahin, the ethnically affiliated Team Africa consistently garnered the largest allegiance from non-ethnic Somali Africans in the student body. At an early match against a team of mixed Latino students, fans of the competing teams clustered in the end zones. The day's earlier match had delivered a 3–1 win to the ethnic Somalis over the Mexican team, so the sidelines were full of disinterested Somalis and Mexicans. When Team Africa scored in the second match, the remaining African population cheered heartily from the end zones, and routinely displayed their loyalty by wearing team colors on tournament days.

Beyond the question of ethnic allegiance within the tournament and the increasing value placed by students on individual skill, the tournament also demonstrated that, within the larger U.S. structure of personal development, sport serves as a way for young people to adopt and model culturally sanctioned values. Put simply, among American men, how a young person conducts himself in sport is an indication of his successful integration of community values. Like the early classroom interactions between Mrs. Morgan and the Somali Bantu students, the controversies of the soccer tournament often illustrated central discrepancies in cultural values between teachers and students, a difference in lifeworld. For example, weeks into the tournament, the ethnic Somalis faced Team Africa in play, and the game ended controversially. Tahlil, the Team Africa goalie and a Somali Bantu teen, successfully blocked an incoming ball, which then rolled back into the goal without the intervention of the opposing team. According to the tournament rules, this would not be considered a goal for the ethnic Somali team because they had not put the ball in play when it rolled backward into the opposing goal. Before the referee and Mr. Jackson were able to call it, the ethnic Somali team, including a player who had already been called out, rushed onto the pitch to argue with the officials. At that point, the officials called the entire team out, and play ended in a tie with Team Africa. This conflict escalated after the call as a number of ethnic Somalis complained bitterly about the result, attempted unsuccessfully to argue with the teachers and tournament officials, and were sent back to their classrooms. For a lot of the student body, and for many players, the tournament was a way of conducting interethnic competition within the school using a play format—soccer.

Interestingly, this goal dispute was also highly frustrating for the U.S.-born male teachers at the school, because they were not reading a larger ethnic competition within the soccer match. Rather, they were reading a failure among the young players to adopt important U.S. cultural values. Venting his frustration about the students, Jackson exclaimed, "They don't know how to behave like sportsmen," a sentiment the normally steady school referee argued had appeared repeatedly throughout the tournament. For most of the U.S.-born teachers, particularly the men, sport is an important avenue for inculcating certain types of values and conduct in boys that eventually demonstrates maturity, an element of sport that Fine (1987) also noted in his study of the role of Little League in the moral development of preadolescent boys. Because these soccer teams were unsupervised by faculty, neither student nor adult group articulated to the other what they perceived as important within the sporting event. For the Somali players, a defeat at the hands of their social inferiors— Somali Bantu and other Africans—was so important that a fight over a call was beyond justifiable; it was necessary. For the male teachers, however, the unsportsmanlike behavior violated some of the most central U.S. cultural norms by which they operate, and by transgressing it, the players forfeited their right to play. This small conflict illustrated a central tournament conundrum: while male faculty saw it as an opportunity for students to achieve success through athletic prowess and culturally sanctioned team values, new students—in this case the bulk of the student population—used it as an opportunity to reinforce ethnic identity.

Over time, however, the trend toward interethnic integration in team selection and nonsectarian sportsmanship indicates that the overarching movement for students is away from affiliation based solely on ethnic identity to affiliation based on individual merit, the same pattern happening in the organization of classrooms based on staging. The two most integrated teams in the tournament were also the two best teams, and they were formed by students who had been at McGuffey for a number of years, and had adopted the qualities of sportsmanship prized by their teachers. Yet, despite their successes on the field, these teams were not fan favorites because they did not have an automatic ethnic base of loyalty. The ethnically affiliated teams could draw on that, particularly from the most recently arrived students. Over time in the school system, however, students became increasingly attracted to winning, and as they did, they turned away from ethnic teams to those based on skill.

A Uniquely American Rite of Passage

So far, this chapter has attempted to demonstrate how the rubrics of the U.S. educational system gradually create an alternative model of identity for teenage Somali Bantu refugees. This model, which coexists with well-entrenched Somali Bantu models, is one based on individual achievement rather than age group, gender, and ethnic affiliation, which are the groupings reinforced by traditional rites of passage into adulthood. I want to end this chapter with a discussion of the very clearly defined rite of passage that reinforces these American cultural values, the State Graduation Test mandated by NCLB, and an exploration of how the administration of the test mirrors the operation of traditional rites of passage into adulthood. Because the passage of the law is relatively recent, there have been few qualitative studies done to assess its impact in the classroom (Valenzuela, Prieto, and Hamilton 2007). My aim here is not to critique its value as a pedagogical tool overall as other scholars have done (Price 2003); rather, it is to attempt to describe its role as a ritual of status change, and to understand that impact on identity formation among these Somali Bantu students within this particular educational setting.

I encountered the formal administration of the SGT twice during my field experience at the High School Welcome Center. The first was in early March, when all tenth graders across the state take the test in their schools. I arrived at McGuffey expecting to attend a normal assortment of lab classes to observe Somali Bantu students. Instead, what I found was that this administration of the test moved the school out of its normal operating routine in a number of ways that mirror Victor Turner's (1969) description of liminality during the ritual process. First, students taking the test were segregated from those in other classes and restricted to their testing rooms throughout the weeklong administration. Although the test was completed with a pencil and testing book, the initiates were relegated to the computer lab, where they could be more easily monitored by those proctoring the exam. Cardboard barriers were erected between seats at the lab, and students were forbidden from any form of talking because, in a school where it is possible to share answers in twenty different languages, all talking is potentially cheating. As ESL students, these initiates had all day to complete their daily tests, so lunch was brought to them from the cafeteria, and they were kept in the testing room to further limit their ability to share information about the test. All excursions to the lavatories and offices were monitored, since testing was also ongoing at MAHS. Although, in the context of the test, the strict protocols of isolation had a pragmatic purpose, it is particularly striking how these painstaking efforts to prevent contamination of the testing environment mirror ritual patterns of isolation in liminality, in which the status and property of the initiates are removed, and they are required to obey instructors or risk severe punishment (Turner 1969, 103). At the welcome center, test-takers/ initiates become nonpersons within the school system, neither participating in ordinary life nor allowed to interact with their peers (Turner 1967, 97), and the efforts to protect the test from contamination underscore Douglas's observation that disorder symbolizes danger to the existing order, in this case, the testing regime ([1966] 2002). Second, even for the students in lab classes, the school schedule was modified because teachers were prioritized for monitoring in the testing room. Class schedules were modified to meet the needs of the initiates, and there was an inversion of their ordinary traffic patterns throughout the week, as lab students did not change classrooms in order to prevent extraneous noise from disturbing the test-takers. During the testing week, teachers moved through the hallways during changes in class, dislocating themselves from their ordinary base of operations and moving instead to meet their students. This radical inversion, in this case in the pattern of movement based on status hierarchy, is another characteristic of the liminal phase in the rites of passage (Turner 1967, 97).

The following September, Linmoor was similarly disrupted by a practice version of the SGT. Under state law, ninth graders have to take practices of the SGT in the autumn. Because all students at the Welcome Center—even those in lab classes—are enrolled as ninth-grade students, every student was required to take a practice version of the test in the new facility. As I noted earlier, the move to Linmoor created a more structured environment at the school, and in this environment, there was a much more explicit discussion of the test and its importance with all students than there had been at the McGuffey facility. When students raised complaints that they were being held back in lab classes, for example, I noted earlier that they were given the opportunity to take a released version of the writing portion of the SGT to prove they could be advanced to normal coursework. In most cases, this successfully quelled further complaints. During the autumn practice run of the SGT, the everyday routine of the school was suspended as it had been during the March administration, although the lack of an actual initiate group meant that the practices of separation and liminality were not as clearly defined as they had been when contamination was a legitimate danger.

Beyond these ritual elements evident in the school, if not in some ways because of them, Somali Bantu students have increasingly come to see the SGT as a rite of passage, indicating that success on it would provide them with the credentials to pursue further study or find better-paying jobs. Early in my fieldwork, Ms. Hegde, whose own background as part of an immigrant Indian family made her more sensitive to unstated cultural difference within diaspora, opined that the Somali Bantu students may never be successful on the SGT because it had not replaced their own ways of measuring success. She felt that, because these students did not necessarily count individual success as important, this constant, looming threat of the SGT was probably useless, despite its consequences for them, the school, and their teachers. She observed that the students were in school because their peers were in school, and peers stick together. However, as the school year progressed, with its deconstructing and restructuring of peer groups based on individual merit and testable progress, the SGT grew in student consciousness. The advanced lab class students began expressing fear about it as early as the first classroom sort, and Ibraahin, who was then attending standard ninth-grade classes, questioned me with great concern about whether he would be allowed to get his diploma if he failed it. By the summer, Maryan and Dahabo demonstrated a sense of futility about ever passing it and getting a decent job, and by autumn, the three Hagarlas in normal ninth-grade classes were grilling me about my experience as a test-taker/initiate, and asking for tips on being successful. After a year of forming and re-forming peer groups based on individual academic achievement, many students had moved from being unaware of the SGT and its consequences to being concerned enough about passing it to seek help from individuals who had successfully completed the passage to adulthood.

It remains to be seen how these students will fare on the SGT as they move into tenth-grade classes and are required to experience this uniquely American rite of passage for the record. For many Somali Bantu students, the experience of U.S. schools has been frustrating, and their lack of progress has discouraged many of their teachers and administrators. Most faculty members do not have much expectation that the Somali Bantu students will pass it. But the acceptance of its impending administration is, in some way, an indication of progress by these student and teachers. Beyond what they learn about math, science, social studies, reading, and writing, the school system has provided these students with an alternate way of constructing adult identity in the United States, through work and individual achievement. The most successful students are learning how to integrate it with other cultural models.

Conclusion

In the early twentieth century, Freudian psychoanalyst Ernst Blum pointed out the correlation between the exams and initiation rituals, arguing that "what serves among primitive peoples as a test of bodily sexual maturity corresponds to [European] examinations for mental maturity" (1926, 467). While his understanding of initiation ritual is far too simplistic, it seems that the testing regime imposed by No Child Left Behind has indeed created an ultimate ritual event in the intellectual development of high school students. For Somali Bantu teenagers, this ritual event caps an alternate system of identity construction, one that is based on individual achievement rather than group identity. It is important to note that, at the time of my initial research with these teenagers, no Somali Bantu student had successfully completed the new rite of passage. However, what is significant is that these students increasingly began to see this passage as important in their own progress toward adult status. As will be clear in the chapter that follows, the American rites of passage have not wholly supplanted more traditional markers for the achievement of adult identity. However, the integration of Somali Bantu students into the U.S. school system, its rituals, and its systems of identification has created an important alternative system of identity and status change.

6

Celebrating Adulthood

Wedding Ritual and the Celebration of Identity

So far, this research study has aimed to explore the experience of adolescence as lived by a group of young Somali Bantu refugees resettling in the United States. To do this, I have concentrated on the everyday practices of these teenagers, their lives within Wedgewood Village Apartments, their consumption of Nigerian videos and World Wrestling Entertainment, and their experience of American rites of passage at the High School Welcome Center. My overarching concern with these elements of identity construction has been to explore what elements of their resettlement lives serve Somali Bantu refugees in the construction of identity as their traditional rituals of initiation become disrupted through dislocation and resettlement. All of the elements of everyday life previously described provide these young refugees and the surrounding elders with tools to influence the process of becoming adults in a context that has radically altered traditional ritual practice. However, as Noyes has noted, people demonstrate identity not just in how they act in the everyday practice but also in the extraordinary events of their cultural world. Group identity also asserts itself in collective performance, in repeated and formalized collective action that manages to conflate individual feeling with collective participation (Noyes 2003, 29–30), which is why, at this point, I want to turn back to ritual practice itself.

This chapter will consider the collective ritual performance of weddings within the diasporic Somali Bantu community precisely because this emerging form so definitively combines the individual experience of passage in the life course with collective participation in the ritual event. To that end, there are two significant themes that emerge from Somali Bantu wedding celebrations. First, in the absence of public practice of initiation ritual and, as a result of the extended adolescence that young people now experience within the school system, weddings have emerged as a critical life cycle event signaling the beginning of adulthood for most Somali Bantu youths. However, it is a passage fraught with considerable ambivalence. Second, beyond what happens within the life course of the individual youth, weddings have become the central event in which the community engages in the performance of expressive culture. Both in person, and through the circulation of videotape, weddings allow the diasporic Somali Bantu community to reaffirm and practice their cultural heritage, and have become the central collective performance in resettlement that allows for the assertion of group cultural identity. Stern and Cicala argue that the "symbols of ethnicity are not merely products of ethnic culture but are solutions to problematic situations that characterize, project, and parody everyday life" (1991, xiii). In this case, wedding celebrations provide an opportunity to assert group identity in the midst of dislocation and resettlement.

The Attainment of Adulthood

As a rite of passage, weddings have become the central milestone marking the successful achievement of adulthood in the life cycle of young Somali Bantu refugees. For the individual teenager, the contracting of a marriage signals that he or she will soon create a separate household and family unit, and thereby progress in status as an adult within the community. In the course of my fieldwork, this status change happened at an earlier age for the girls than for the boys. None of the young men I came to know indicated that their betrothal had been contracted yet, or was even contemplated while they were still in high school. Yet, for their female counterparts, the attainment of a marriage contract increasingly became a focus of their teenage lives. Across households and ethnic differences, a consistent pattern of marriage contracting became evident over the course of my field experience. The process begins when a young man from the diasporic Somali Bantu community gains the financial ability to support a wife. At that point, he approaches the family of a young woman he is interested in marrying and makes them an offer of a bride-price, which serves three functions. First, it is an indication that the suitor can provide a home separate from that of his parents, although it is typically within the public housing project that accommodates his family and the local Somali Bantu community. Second, it compensates her family for removing her labor from them. Finally, it demonstrates that the suitor can support the young woman as a wife and mother.

According to community members, resettlement has had particular effects on determining bride-price. All of the elements described have become more expensive in the United States, so bride-prices have risen in comparison to those negotiated in Africa. In addition, the bride-price must be offered in a lump sum of U.S. currency here, rather than in a combination of currency, goods, and trade that would have been more acceptable before resettlement. However, despite these changes within resettlement, the system of contracting has remained central to organizing Somali Bantu marriages, and for the generation of young women in high school during my fieldwork experience, marriage remains the path to a future independent of their families of origin. In my discussions with the teenage girls, for example, there was virtually no mention of delaying marriage to complete high school, although there was some consideration of delaying pregnancy to achieve that goal. Ultimately, among the girls, marriage proposals are analogous to receiving a job offer, a perspective that is shared with other African groups. In her work on Sudan, Boddy describes marriage as the inauguration of male and female social careers, in that through it, "a man acquires access to his wife's fertility, and she, the means to activate it" (1982, 688). In fact, at the High School Welcome Center, most of the teenage girls who had become engaged were significantly more secure about their futures than those who had not, and their approach to marriage echoed Boddy's analysis.

At the welcome center, engagement news was not typically circulated between teachers and students. However, as the first academic year of my fieldwork drew to a close, rumors began to circulate among teachers that Timiro, a sixteen-year-old intermediate female student, was planning to be married over the summer. Initially, Timiro was reluctant to confirm her wedding with me or any other person from outside the Somali Bantu community, and my first questions to her were met not with answers but with more questions from Timiro, who pretended to be anxious about how I had heard her news, and asked me to name my sources. Her efforts to deflect me were sabotaged by her girlfriends, and eventually her male classmates, who were delighted to confirm that she was indeed getting married within a week of the close of the school year. So, while many of the teenagers happily invited me to attend the celebration and shared details about its date and time, Timiro continued to obfuscate, divulging no specifics about her big event.

In fact, Timiro's news opened up a new and somewhat convoluted line of inquiry with the teenagers, who demonstrated considerable ambivalence toward the attainment of this milestone in the life course. On the one hand, most of the students were happy to share information about the engagements of their peers, and I learned that Timiro was not the only female student at the school who was planning a wedding. For the Somali Bantu students generally, the impending wedding of one of their peer group was a happily anticipated community event, and they were eager to have me come to the celebrations, which had been arranged as far as three years into the future. On an individual level, however, no teenage girl was willing to discuss her own betrothal, even as her friends shared detailed information and expressed delight about it. Timiro's model of obfuscation was not an individual one; it was a habit shared by all girls preparing for marriage. Further, despite the delight many teenagers demonstrated at the prospect of one of their peers marrying, the achievement of this new status in the life course brought a new pressure for both the boys and girls within the age group.

Boys Anticipating Marriage

For the teenage boys still in high school, there was no opportunity to marry at this point in the life cycle, because they needed to demonstrate financial independence and security in order to begin the process of contracting a marriage. The beginning of the marriage process among their female agemates noticeably increased the pressure on them to seek employment. As the girls began to contemplate the establishment of their own households, and the pool of familiar and available Somali Bantu girls began to shrink, their status as boys and not men became increasingly uncomfortable. There was, for example, little enthusiasm among them for the impending wedding celebrations of any of the engaged girls in their age group. When I asked individually, none of Timiro's male contemporaries was certain he would attend her wedding, which was a marked contrast to the enthusiasm shown by her female contemporaries and most adult members of the community. In fact, further private discussions indicated that many of the boys felt her wedding was a mistake because of her young age. Heybe, who boldly claimed that he had dated Timiro prior to her engagement, expressed bitterness toward Mohamed, her twentysomething fiancé. In this case, the bitterness seemed to stem less from any particular romantic feelings for Timiro than for a jealousy at the ability of her fiancé to establish himself successfully as an adult. Likewise, later in the summer, both Ibraahin and Tahlil openly condemned the marriage to me, which they felt had been forced on Timiro by the difficult domestic situation she endured at Wedgewood.

Timiro, it should be noted, lived in an apartment with her father and his wife, a woman many believed had caused the sudden death of Timiro's mother in Nairobi prior to resettlement. It was not that people believed she had murdered Timiro's mother, who was held in high esteem by most members of the community; rather, shortly after Timiro's father married this new wife, her mother had contracted a sudden fever and died in Nairobi's publicly funded

Kenyatta Hospital. The cause of death was attributed to malaria, a source that is often blamed for sudden sickness and death in East Africa when there are no resources for further medical inquiry. But this death, coming without warning just as the family was preparing to move to the United States, was blamed on the new wife, and she was generally treated with suspicion by the rest of the community. To be sure, on my visits to Wedgewood, Timiro seemed markedly more comfortable in the homes of her sisters than the home of her father, and I was discouraged from visiting her there. According to Tahlil and Ibraahin, her marriage had been contracted by adults in pursuit of their own interests, and the boys expressed concern that her husband would not treat her well, and that she would soon move back to Wedgewood, divorced, perhaps pregnant or with small children, where she would have to fend for herself without even a high school education since her father and stepmother were entitled to her bride-price.

Apart from their concerns for this particular match, the teenage boys expressed very little interest in their own marriage prospects, but became increasingly focused on achieving financial independence. I have noted in a previous chapter Ibraahin's repeated discussions with me about finding long-term employment. While he was the most vocal about it, his concerns were increasingly a mirror of my discussions with other members of his peer group. As males, their path to adulthood requires them to seek financial independence before achieving physical independence. Over the course of their high school experience, there was a noticeable shift in the way many of the boys perceived this path to the future, and some had begun to plot very attainable routes to finding long-term employment. Ibraahin had begun his trade course and found a job mowing lawns, for example, while Tahlil had set his sights on becoming a policeman and was honing his athletic skills in the hope of receiving scholarship money for college like another young man in the community. For both boys, finishing high school was the first and necessary step to achieving their long-term goals, and they became increasingly committed to succeeding at school and on the SGT. This seriousness of purpose, while not accompanied by a formal ritual event, nevertheless demonstrated a move to some kind of higher plateau of maturity, and was often rewarded by school officials with special responsibilities that elevated their status at school. In contrast, some of their peers, like Heybe and Haaruun, continued to operate with a vision of the future that involved less wholesome skills, like thieving. Still others, like Mahdi and Hanad, had not yet set pragmatic goals and were still perceived as childlike by their teachers. In the eyes of the Somali Bantu community, these boys were all peers, but their ability to move into adulthood depended on them taking the first steps to setting up an independent household, and that meant a plan for financial independence.

Girls Anticipating Marriage

Meanwhile, among the teenage girls, the imperative to marry grew increasingly louder. Conversation turned routinely to betrothal rumors and news, and it became increasingly clear that the sixteen- and seventeen-year-olds were at their peak on the marriage market. Even fourteen-year-old Haajiro insisted that she was already engaged to somebody she met during her brief stay in Nairobi, a man whom she claimed was busy raising her bride-price. Months later, after a semester of attending a mainstream high school, she admitted that she was just beginning on the market, where her prospects were just starting to emerge, and, as they seemed bright, Haajiro seemed to grow in self-confidence. By contrast, seventeen-year-old Maryan began to openly express her disenchantment with cultural restrictions placed on her through marriage. Soon after Timiro's wedding, Maryan began to opine that she did not want to marry because she did not want to have a bunch of kids to look after and piles of diapers to change. This bitter comment came during an afternoon in which she had been drafted by her elder sisters to watch a large collection of their children while the married women gathered to celebrate another bride. It was not the first time one of the young girls had said this to me. In fact, two of Maryan's preteen nieces had both congratulated me on my own unmarried status during one of my home visits and indicated that they too did not want to change diapers for most of their adult lives. But that generation of younger students, who have virtually no memory of Africa and have spent an entire childhood in American schools and consuming American media, are far more fluent in American language usage and popular culture and are dramatically more successful at integrating the surrounding culture into their personal lives. There is a noticeable difference in cultural practice between Maryan's agemates and those of her preteen nieces, and I believe her complaint about diapers that day was based more on her disappointments on the marriage market than it was on any particular desire to be an independent American woman. In fact, as members of her age group continued to prove more successful attracting the attention of marriageable Somali Bantu men, and subsequently contracting to marry them, Maryan became increasingly disparaging of her own community. In the absence of any interest by Somali Bantu men, she became increasingly insistent that she did not like them, and wanted to marry a white man or find a job and look after herself.

Her concerns were shared by community elders as well. When I asked her parents, Abuukar and Basra, about Maryan's marriage plans, her parents explained with some concern that no young man had yet approached Abuukar to arrange a marriage with Maryan. In my previous questions about Maryan's future, this subject had been routinely dismissed with laughter. However, in the wake of Timiro's wedding, it was obvious that this was a source of concern, since her future well-being depends on her marrying and setting up her own household. Although Abuukar and Basra have encouraged their children and grandchildren to succeed at school—Basra's son Maahir is among the first in the community to receive a high school diploma—adulthood requires the young to establish their own households, a step that requires marriage for both the boys and the girls. In fact, the two elements of financial independence and marriage are so interlinked that Maahir's academic success had created a situation that furthered the social impetus for him to marry rather than diminished it. He had received a full scholarship to play soccer at a local university, and it included accommodation on campus. To the college, this accommodation would allow Maahir to base himself close to academic resources and help him succeed as an athlete and student. To his family, independent accommodation meant that Maahir was in a position to find a wife, and they had begun assessing his prospects within the larger Somali Bantu community. There was no expectation that Maahir would bring a wife into his dormitory, but by creating a separate household, he was expected to find and install his bride into his portion of the apartment he currently shared with his sister Aasiya and her daughter. Ironically, the outcome that the university intended—to provide Maahir with the space to succeed in college—would result in a myriad of distractions as he and the community prepared to establish him as a successful adult.

Meanwhile, no marriage prospects emerged for Maryan as the official American demarcation of adulthood, her eighteenth birthday, drew closer, and she became increasingly isolated from her peers. By late summer, Maryan began telling her friends that she was dating an American boy of about her own age and, later in the fall, she indicated that their relationship had progressed to the point where he had given her a cell phone, an important relationship milestone shared by girls in her peer group who had become betrothed. Of course, she explained, the phone had been confiscated by her parents, whom she claimed had threatened to kick her out of the house, called the police on the young man, and refused to feed her if she did not cut off contact with her American suitor. She expected to be thrown out of the house when she turned eighteen in a few months' time. When I asked her if she wanted to be with this American boy, she shrugged her shoulders. I got the same response when I asked her if she liked him back. However, when I asked her if she likes that he wants to be with her, she smiled widely and said yes.

I must admit that, from the first, I was skeptical about the actual existence of this young man. Maryan's English was highly limited, making her claims that they had met and corresponded online difficult to believe. Likewise, between her duties within her large coterie of family and friends, the demands of school, and the social restrictions placed on teenage girls, Maryan had very little free-dom of movement to coordinate a romance with an outsider. Finally, when her narrative reached the point where she expected to be homeless, she often added a suggestion that she move into my home and offered to provide domestic labor in exchange for living there. I was not certain if the story was being contrived specifically for me, or how deep it reached into other circles of her world. Her half-nephew Mahdi, who lived in the family home and attended the same school, indicated that there was no fighting between Maryan and his grand-parents. Late in the fall term, she wrote about this matter in a school essay, which was flagged by one of the teachers for investigation by the school psychologist. Her investigations confirmed that the romance was a fantasy created by Maryan, a way of constructing an escape from the pressures of Somali Bantu pre-adulthood, and her own disappointment on the marriage market.

Ambivalence and Affirmation

I noted earlier that Erik Erikson (1959) theorized that individual identity is a sense of continuity that develops over time with the overcoming of obstacles and an individual's desires. In his thinking, sociocultural surroundings provide guidance and support to lessen the stress of development, often providing a space that allows for exploration within a developmental stage, which he called a psychosocial moratorium. Without this guidance, the individual becomes lost, particularly if the obstacle becomes insurmountable and meaningless. School and liminal periods within initiation rituals both serve as moratoria. In this case, the rising influence of the former and the disrupted practice of the latter contribute to the ambivalence toward marriage I observed in my research. On the one hand, the approach of marriage as a milestone in the Somali Bantu life course promises adult status, something that has been delayed and confused by the disruption of initiation ritual in flight and resettlement. On the other hand, the surrounding U.S. culture has provided a model of adulthood and financial independence based on education. For the girls, the disruption to education caused by marriage and pregnancy is obvious, but it is no less considerable for the boys. The heightened significance of marriage causes them to focus on obtaining employment as early as possible, often at low-paying jobs. These jobs are attractive because they provide the hope of adult status and its privileges. However, the surrounding U.S. culture provides the hope of even greater privileges, leaving these teenagers uncertain how to proceed toward their futures.

Regardless of the ambivalence toward marriage among the teenage refugees, in diaspora, where the rites of initiation have become increasingly difficult to maintain as practiced in the village, marriage has become the central ritual marking the passage into adulthood for young members of the community. In his discussion of the equator-crossing narrative within the crossing-the-line ritual of the U.S. Navy, Simon Bronner notes that it "has the manifest function of inculcating separate (or tribal) cultural values and obedience to a select group's mores and institutions. It has the latent function of addressing an essential ambivalence—tensions created by a male dominated world with female norms" (2006, 27). The emerging wedding ritual demonstrates a similar dual nature within the diasporic Somali Bantu community. Like the equator-crossing narrative, the manifest function of the wedding ritual is to establish young men and women as (re)productive adults within the community, and in doing so it also inculcates cultural values and demonstrates obedience to the group's mores and institutions. I would also suggest that its very public and celebratory nature also serves a latent function, to address the ambivalence many young people have toward this particular institution and the traditional practices surrounding it. As the Somali Bantu community becomes increasingly entrenched within the U.S. landscape, weddings have adopted characteristics of their U.S. counterparts. As will be clear in the description that follows, some of these characteristics involve fairly superficial adaptations, such as the rental of a hall or the wearing of Western-style wedding clothes. However, the manner in which these celebrations place young people at the center of community attention is a more significant characteristic shared by both cultures, and like their American counterparts, playing the central role in such a public display of cultural form helps to resolve some of the ambivalence many young people increasingly feel toward this life passage.

Weddings have become the central celebratory event of the Somali Bantu community, and the importance of these celebrations is not limited to passages through individual life courses. The marriage ritual has also become a central venue for displaying and celebrating a greater communal cultural identity as Somali Bantu. The collective adult enthusiasm for weddings—whether experienced in person or through videotape—underscores how weddings have become the central occasion in which the larger community celebrates its cultural identity. To illustrate, I will describe Timiro's wedding specifically and then discuss evolving patterns of celebrating Somali Bantu weddings and their larger cultural significance in the midst of resettlement.

A Wedding at Wedgewood

As it became apparent in the waning days of the school year that adults from outside the Somali Bantu community knew that one of the students was marrying, many of the teenagers began to discuss the subject of marriage openly. Timiro had been engaged for a while, and her wedding date was well known within the community at Wedgewood, as were the impending weddings of Dahabo and Hagarla, two other teenage girls at the high school whose weddings were then in the planning stages. All three girls were coy about their plans when asked directly about them, but their agemates and families were not. In fact, at Wedgewood, the dates for these weddings were widely circulated, and I was issued an open invitation by many adult members of the community to attend the festivities of each, despite the brides' refusals to confirm any of these details. Ultimately, Timiro relented in her determined silence, and invited me and other interested members of the faculty to come to the housing project on the Saturday following the end of the school year to celebrate her wedding.

My teenage informants instructed me to come directly to Wedgewood around 9 p.m. on the day of the wedding to participate in it. However, when I arrived at Wedgewood in the mid-afternoon, I found the housing project already given over to celebration. With the news that a wedding was happening within the local community, other Somali Bantu refugees had begun to arrive from cities within a six-hour radius by car. By the time I arrived at Maryan's home, I found her already removed with Timiro and other bridesmaids, and Abuukar and Basra's apartment full of unfamiliar people. There was a collection of heavily perfumed women, dressed in shiny, elegant clothes. Most wore a co-ordinated ensemble consisting of a stiff underskirt peeking out from under a formless light overdress made of more decorative fabric, topped by a matching headscarf and shawl. The overdresses were simply cut swaths of colorful fabric sewn together to form a large square with head and arm holes, which they then draped across their bodies. In addition, most women were adorned in an assort-ment of gold-plated earrings, necklaces, and bracelets. In contrast to her sumptuously dressed guests, Basra was in her day clothes preparing food for a

Somali Bantu women celebrating Timiro's wedding, June 2008. Photo by author.

group of men from Pittsburgh who were based at her home for the weekend. Soon after I arrived, she produced plates of food for them and her husband, Abuukar, who delighted in this opportunity to introduce me to their traditional foods. A plate of fish served with cooked spaghetti noodles circulated, and the men sat on the floor and wound the pasta in their hands before taking a piece of the fish and placing the whole handful in their mouths, sharing the plate among one another. Next came a plate of ugali and mabamia, a dish of corn flour combined with fried okra that was a favorite of Abuukar's. By the time the men began to eat, the women had all left to visit other homes, leaving me the sole adult woman in a room full of male guests and small children. Despite my offers to help with the food, Basra and Abuukar insisted I sit with the children as the visiting men answered my questions about the celebration.

Like many of the visitors, the men from Pittsburgh were not personally known to Timiro, but they had connections with the groom and Abuukar from their time together in refugee camps. This pattern recurred throughout the housing complex. Visitors had arrived from the larger Somali Bantu world, and the community at Wedgewood provided them with food and a place to sleep, apartment by apartment. One of the visitors from Pittsburgh noted that while many Somali Bantu refugees may work in hotels, they never stay in them. They stay with other Somali Bantu refugees. In actual fact, the celebrations had already started at Wedgewood as the population of Somali Bantu swelled for the weekend. At the formal reception hall, there would be no need for the bride and groom to offer their guests a meal; the women of Wedgewood were already producing it in individual living rooms across the compound. As they ate, discussion soon turned to other weddings, over which the adults felt a sense of community ownership. The wedding ritual, while a contract between two individuals, seemed more important as an arrangement with the larger community, an event in which everybody had a sense of ownership.

Back at their apartment, the afternoon was turning to early evening. Timiro, Maryan, and the other teenage girls who were part of her entourage had been removed to a separate location earlier to prepare for the wedding, and Basra had tasked Mahdi to take me to her daughter Aasiya to locate the bridal party. Our effort to find them was considerable. First, Mahdi and I picked our way through various crowded Somali Bantu apartments to find Aasiya. Once we located her, she and I and a group of her agemates moved back across the Wedgewood compound seeking information on the location of the young girls. It was a hot summer day, and as meals ended inside the crowded apartments, visitors spilled out into the common spaces of the Wedgewood compound. There was little evidence that day that any group aside from the Somali Bantu lived at Wedgewood Village, as older men hung out under trees digesting their meals, and women walked around displaying their finery and reconnecting with extended family, friends, and former neighbors in Somalia and the camps. Dorothy Noyes (2003) has noted that, while community may be a social imaginary, that does not render it insignificant, as it requires bodies gathering together and sharing experience. In this instance, as bodies crowded into tiny apartment spaces and eventually out into Wedgewood's common spaces, it became clear that the whole community at Wedgewood was putting on this wedding, that the event was significant not because of Timiro or Mohamed personally but because it provided a space for the far-flung community members to come together.

Preparing the Bride

Eventually, we located Timiro and her bridesmaids, who had been sequestered at the apartment of an ethnic Somali family a few miles away. When I first arrived there, the teenage girls seemed to be completely unsupervised, and were playing Indian music videos loudly on their host's television while they touched up henna designs on their legs and arms. A henna artist had applied the initial designs with a fast-drying compound, which allowed the teenagers some freedom of movement but also required them to reapply to bring out greater darkness. Deborah Kapchan has noted that the slow-drying application of henna in Moroccan pre-wedding celebrations renders the bride immobile, which forces her to fast, and increases her awareness of her own body, allowing the beautification process to act as a celebration of the sexual body and as a means of incorporating grace, or baraka, into the celebration (1993, 31). Among these Somali Bantu girls, however, the fast-drying henna and Indian dance music eliminated any sacred potential in this ritual of body adornment. Instead, the girls sang along, talked of boys and love, and jumped to their feet to dance when Somali disco music played from a boom box. In imitation of the dancing of older, married members of the community that they had observed at other weddings or on videotape, the teenagers tied cloths around their waists and competed to see who could wiggle their hips and bottoms most effectively. Throughout the dancing, Timiro sat serenely on the couch laughing at the antics of her friends. Because her mother was not there, her father had arranged for a wedding planner to manage the details of her wedding. The woman he chose was not a member of the Somali Bantu community, but a Barawan, an ethnic group from the Somali coast with a history of mixed cultural ancestry similar to the Swahili communities of Kenya, Tanzania, and Mozambique. This wedding planner had the assistance of her two daughters and a niece, who helped her with the henna work, hair, and makeup. She had further enlisted an ethnic Somali friend to provide this apartment as a secluded location for the preparation of the wedding party. Together, the assembled group provided a picture of Somalia's multicultural diaspora. This use of a wedding planner seemed to be an unusual element for Somali Bantu weddings, and this forceful woman seemed to be making all the decisions for Timiro. She had picked out the dress, and her daughters were responsible for the styling of the bride and her party. After controversies over hair extensions and Timiro's dress, the teenagers began to view her presence as an extension of Timiro's bad luck in losing her mother at such a young age.

Just before midnight, the dress was delivered to Timiro. It was a rented white American-style bridal gown in satin and lace with a halter top that revealed all of Timiro's arms and much of her shoulders and back. This traditionally Western style dress is a post-resettlement innovation. Earlier in the evening, Aasiya had pulled out photos from her wedding, which had taken place in the refugee camps of northern Kenya. In them, she wore a colored dress in the style of most of Timiro's wedding guests, with a corresponding head covering. It was significantly less elaborate than what is available in the United States and revealed less skin. The wedding planner had selected this same Somali Bantu style for Timiro's bridesmaids. In this case, these light overdresses looked like they had swirls of foil in the fabric design, and they were paired with a matching solid underskirt. They too had been selected by the wedding planner and were provided to the teenage girls in packages of peach, brown, or red ensembles, which included elaborate, gold-plated jewelry. Like Timiro, they wore high-heeled sandals, and the hennaed decorations on their feet and legs occasionally poked out from under their stiff underskirts. This decision to dress in closer conformity to women elders is contrary to the growing trend in the Somali Bantu community to wear American-style formal wear as part of the celebrations. As a result, there was a mixed reaction to them from the teens in this wedding party, who had turned on the wedding planner and found fault with most of her aesthetic decisions as the evening wore on.

By the time they finished styling, some of the girls wore hair extensions, others wore wigs, while others had their hair straightened, then curled stylishly. This was the first time in my experience of them that the Somali Bantu teens wore no hair coverings. Meanwhile, Timiro had been dressed in her rented white gown. Although it was a bit large on her, everyone agreed that it, the hair extensions, veil, jewelry, and elaborate makeup made her look beautiful. Were

Timiro in her wedding finery, June 2008. Photo by author.

it not for the occasional view of her hennaed feet poking out from high-heeled sandals at the base of her dress, she would have appeared completely assimilated into the aesthetics of American life. After the hours of preparation, anxiety over her hair and makeup, frenetic dancing by her friends, and constant reminders of her mother's absence, Timiro managed a few proud smiles about her appearance. Around 1 a.m., a group of Somali Bantu women elders arrived with a driver to collect the wedding party.

The Reception

Before the wedding, I asked a number of young girls about what to expect from the wedding ritual itself. All of these questions produced no concrete answers. In fact, most of us were familiar with the formal aspects of Somali Bantu weddings because of the widespread circulation of wedding videos throughout the refugee community. Because these receptions have become an important ritual event, videotapes of them are hugely popular within the larger diasporic Somali Bantu community, where they circulate around individual households across the country. At some point in nearly all my visits to Somali Bantu homes, my hosts have put a wedding video into the VCR and have sat to watch it with me at considerable length, and there has recently been a surge of such videos uploaded onto YouTube, although this activity was not a part of my field experience. It was highly unusual for the family watching the videotapes to have any personal connection to anyone recorded on camera, but that never dampened their enthusiasm for circulating and watching these videos. In all of these weddings, there seemed to be little in the way of formal ritual. Rather, there was typically a formal presentation of the bride and groom, followed by extensive and exuberant dancing by senior members of the community. Timiro, the first among her peer group to be married, could not tell me if there would be vows, although she said she expected to sign something.

By the time the girls arrived at the reception hall, it was after 1 a.m., and the guests had already been celebrating long before their arrival. Timiro, her face covered in a Western tulle veil, was escorted around the hall by her groom, Mohamed. Two elaborate upholstered chairs had been set up near a multi-tiered cake decorated with white and yellow frosting. Timiro and Mohamed circled their guests in a deliberate manner and then took their seats on the two thrones to watch the celebrations. First, her wedding party of teenage girls lined up together to dance in formation. Despite their boisterous dancing during preparations, the teenage girls were now very subdued. Maryan remarked later that, although she loves to dance, she felt very shy in front of all the guests. This feeling seemed to be shared by her companions, as all of them focused their eyes on the ground and moved stiffly side to side using mostly their legs and feet, rather than demonstrating the hip thrusts of elders as they had done earlier in the evening. Not only were their movements limited but all of the girls, including Timiro, wore very solemn expressions and seemed perfectly miserable about the event, which was also a dramatic contrast to their exuberance earlier in the evening. Soon, the male members of the wedding party, who, like Mohamed, seemed to be in their early twenties, lined up across from the girls to dance. Mohamed was dressed in all-white formal wear, including tails, a bow tie, and a cummerbund. His party of young men also wore Western-style formal wear in black and white, although their ensembles did not include tails or ties but white shirts buttoned to the neck, a growing trend in U.S. formal wear. In this short dance performance, they too moved side to side in formation opposite the girls, although with a bit less discomfort at performing. There were no pairs dancing, just two lines of young people attempting to keep formation while the girls kept their faces focused intently on the floor.

Soon, this somewhat awkward dancing ended, and the guests began to join in. From this point, there were two kinds of wedding dances. In the first, guests danced to traditional music in gendered groups, with elder women in particular enjoying the opportunity to demonstrate their abilities. In the second, teams of younger men, ranging in age from fifteen to thirty, danced in formation to Somali disco music. These teams, who dress in uniform T-shirts and rehearse their choreography before the event, are a new trend in Somali Bantu expressive culture. In the early stages of my research, no wedding videos included such a group. In fact, Timiro's wedding was the first time I had seen this type of dancing. This particular group had formed in the Pittsburgh Somali Bantu community, and its members had traveled to this wedding to perform at this event. By the time my fieldwork ended nine months later, at least one of the male students had begun a similar group in this city and had begun traveling throughout the Midwest for other Somali Bantu weddings. Throughout their performance, guests walked up and stuffed small denominations of cash into their props and hats to reward them. In his tracing of the Beni Ngoma, a type of all-male popular dance form that evolved in Kenya and Tanzania during the colonial period, Terence Ranger (1975) notes that its popularity can be construed in a number of ways, as a means of participating in the modern world as well as a means of integrating premodern cultural forms into an emerging modernity. Like the Beni Ngoma, this emerging dance form has drawn young men into a public dance role within Somali Bantu society, which is a significant break with tradition.

In her ethnographic work on southern Somali communities prior to the collapse of the Somali state, Francesca Declich argued that women had considerable power within the community, largely because of their performance of local history through dance and the ritual power that connected fertility with fortune (1995b, 107). In subsequent studies of the population within the refugee camps, however, she further noted that both the widespread experience of rape and an administrative structure within the camps that presumed male authority served to disempower women and remove them from public space (2000, 43–44). In this case, the two types of dancing alternated. The guests danced spontaneously through one or two pieces of music, then the young male performers danced through a few pieces of choreography. If, in fact, dancing at ritual events was a way for women to express authority in the community, then the evolution of dance practices at weddings bears out the trend of disempowerment that Declich noted in the camps. Further, early in my fieldwork, the wedding videos I witnessed typically showed an alternating pattern of dance that allowed senior women a prominent place in the dancing. This new trend in weddings, in which groups of young men perform in formation, allows the young men to dominate the celebration; the dancing by guests that alternated with it allowed for no prominent display of female dance.

Throughout all this activity, Timiro and Mohamed sat on their thrones watching the festivities. Eventually, women from the community began cutting the cake, and plates were passed around to the guests. The dancing continued until the early morning hours, when the bride and groom circled their guests in the deliberate way they had entered, then departed for their new life together in a different city. The wedding ritual had reached an end. In attempting to analyze this particular rite of passage, it seems particularly noteworthy that there appears to be no tripartite structure of separation, transition, and reincorporation (van Gennep [1909] 1960). To be sure, the bride and groom were removed from the community for an extended period and then reincorporated into the community later. However, there was no ritual of separation, and the transitional, or liminal, space served merely to allow for adornment; it had no instructional purpose. There was no ambiguity or paradox, no sacred symbols, or suspension of hierarchies (Turner 1967). It is arguable that the deliberate circling of the bride and groom into the wedding hall, and later out again, is the sole ritualistic element of the wedding event, and, if it is to be analyzed within the framework of Arnold van Gennep or Victor Turner, it serves as a reincorporation of the married couple into the larger social group in this new identity. For an observer of ritual, this limited ritual structure provides little to analyze. Yet the community was satisfied.

Sally Moore and Barbara Myerhoff have pointed out that, regardless of form or religious/secular context, rituals are expressive acts with operational efficacy that can be considered from their outcomes rather than structure. They suggest five different outcomes for analysis of these rituals. In this case, the wedding ritual had an explicit purpose and affected social relations, and it reinforced the cultural order over the cultural void, three of the five criteria. Ultimately, Timiro and Mohamed emerged as husband and wife within the larger Somali Bantu community. What is more complicated is the ritual's use of explicit symbols or implicit statements, the remaining two outcomes (Moore and Myerhoff 1977, 15–16). This ritual synthesized American and Somali Bantu symbols and expressive traditions, providing an implicit statement of cultural practice in evolution and reinforcing the aesthetic of assemblage noted in the earlier discussion of the emerging village life practiced by the community. Ronald Grimes has argued that, even in relatively stable sociocultural circumstances, rites of passage "are not givens; they are hand-me-downs, quilts we continue to patch" (2000, 12). The wedding ritual in diaspora, with its borrowings of white dresses and cakes, its opportunities to display old and emerging traditions of dance, and its feasting on food and the company of other refugees from a disintegrated state, is indeed a patchwork. Yet it is the patchwork that effectively reinforces and constructs the dual nature of both assemblage and social boundedness of Somali Bantu identity practice demonstrated in everyday life.

Marriage and Its Implications on the Larger Community

Despite its lack of a formalized structure, the ritual of marriage has become fundamental in affirming a distinctive ethnic identity in that it has become a central venue for the public display of expressive culture, an event that allows the community to gather together despite geographic distance, share its stories and food, display traditional adornment (whether through clothing, jewelry, or henna art), and enthusiastically engage in both old and new forms of dancing. The wedding ritual has become so significant, in fact, that it must be shared and circulated in the increasingly wider community through videotape and, increasingly, digital video.

It is not just the main wedding celebration that has become a subject for recording and circulation. Later in the summer of Timiro's wedding, I arrived at Wedgewood to find another wedding celebration going on in the compound, even though the wedding was weeks in the future and happening in Virginia. The mother of the prospective bride had come to visit, so many Somali Bantu women, who could not afford the money or time to travel to that wedding, were holding a preemptive celebration. One of the apartments had been cleared of much of its living room furniture; its windows were deliberately covered with fabric, so that the apartment had turned into a dance hall for the day. A collection of at least fifty adult women had squeezed into it, some cooking traditional food in the small kitchen while others danced boisterously to African popular music. The group of assembled women had all been married themselves, and they danced before an enthusiastic crowd of their peers and a quiet, respectful group of younger, unmarried men, one of whom was videotaping the entire celebration. The camera had been hooked up to a television, so as the women watched themselves, their dancing became more elaborate and they competed over their dancing styles. Although this was a gathering of women who danced in celebration of a ritual event, the popular music and playfully competitive environment seemed to bear little resemblance to Declich's descriptions of women dancing their power in the prediasporic period (1995b). Instead, this was an opportunity for the women to celebrate together without the intrusion of men, a chance to dance and laugh and cook for one another, to celebrate by themselves.

Despite the secluded nature of the party, with participation limited solely to married women, the video capturing the celebration would be given to the bride's mother as a gift, and then circulate around the larger Somali Bantu community, as tapes of other weddings do, allowing the diasporic community to join in the individual celebration. The seemingly private celebration would be turned into an object of expressive culture that would come to influence and reinforce Somali Bantu cultural identity. Felicia McMahon has noted that DiDinga refugees from Sudan record their collectively performed dance as a way to preserve non-Western identity, and that these tapes connect the refugees to their ancestral past as well as the larger diaspora of DiDinga. The use of videotape to circulate the dance performances allows them to be preservers of their own culture, and pushes the performance of expressive culture into new forms (McMahon 2007, 177–78). Greg Gow describes similar video use among diasporic Oromo from Ethiopia, calling these recordings "video libraries" that allow illiterate migrants/refugees to keep records of their personal and collective histories, as well as narrate the arts and events playing onscreen, and thereby move themselves from the margins to the center of events (2002, 87, 89). The circulation of videos within the Somali Bantu community operates in a similar manner. Now that resettlement has allowed them access to video cameras and video players, celebrations are routinely recorded and circulated. As a happy occasion that allows for celebration, weddings are particularly effective in providing opportunities for Somali Bantu refugees to gather together, and connect with their ancestral past. Capturing it on film allows families to gather in mixed-gender and mixed-age groups to watch other Somali Bantu, many of whom are not personally known to them, dance at weddings and birthday parties to both traditional and popular music. The video offers the larger diaspora a chance to participate in expressive culture in multiple locations, and circulation has become so important that cameras are hired even for this rather insignificant and distant celebration of a life cycle event.

Conclusion

As a movement within the life course, most Somali Bantu teenagers exhibit a certain degree of ambivalence toward weddings. For the teen girls, the contracting of marriage offers them a sense of security about their futures, even as it limits that future to traditional roles and indicates that they may face isolation from familiar friends and relations. For the teen boys, arrival at this stage in the life course indicates that their success as adults depends on their ability to support a wife and children, and it similarly creates a conflict between U.S. and Somali Bantu approaches to success. Social psychologists James Coté and Anton Allahar note that how a culture defines coming of age depends on its stability, because as the identity of adult members becomes ambiguous, they are less able to guide young people through the process of forming identity (1996, 71). Ambivalence aside, young people have come to recognize that the shift in identity that accompanies this step in the life course is increasingly the most significant one through which they must pass.

Within the larger Somali Bantu community, there is no ambivalence about weddings. These ever-changing ritual events are the central opportunity to reinforce community identity despite its evolving nature in the midst of diaspora. In her discussion of ritual and group identity, Noyes notes that repetition is a key method by which performance cements identity, arguing that a community "exists in its collective performances: they are the locus of its imagining in their content and of its realization in their performance" (2003, 30). As wedding videos circulate from living room to living room, and out into cyberspace, a sense of group cohesion is continually reinforced, one that is based on improvisation as well as traditional expressive culture, but which serves to connect members of the group with a ritual history and present community.

7

Identities in Development

Culture, Gender, and Life Cycle in Diaspora

$\mathcal{T}$he aim of this book has been to explore how the practices of Somali Bantu teenagers, their community, and their teachers serve to inculcate various elements of identity in resettlement, a context that has disrupted traditional ritual practices of initiation for young members of a community where these practices have historically defined membership within the culture group. To that end, I argued that the aesthetic criteria practiced by the Somali Bantu community in everyday life reinforce an overarching cultural identity based on two differing ideals, one of assemblage in decoration practices and ethnicity within the emerging community and the other of the maintenance of fixed boundaries between genders and group membership that are traditionally reinforced through initiation ritual. Likewise, I argued that these teens have, through patterns of media consumption, developed a complex relationship between the fantasies of their new ethnoscape and traditional gender models that reinforce prediasporic ideas about gender roles and identity, even as it allows for increased membership in the consumerist culture of the surrounding U.S. environment. Finally, I discussed two emerging approaches to achieving status as adults in this context, through completion of education and marriage, both of which reinforce the centrality of financial independence as a marker of adulthood. The first, provided by the school system, encourages individual academic success and status change for both boys and girls through passage of the State Graduation Test. The second reinforces the role of marriage for both boys and girls in affirming their arrival at adulthood within the community.

For the sake of analysis, I have concentrated on three modalities of identity that are central concerns of initiation rituals: group cultural identity, gender, and status within the life cycle. In general, the experience of dislocation and resettlement seems to have had the most immediate effects on the emergence of cultural identity and developmental status, while at this early stage, gender has remained more resistant to change. Before I close this project, I want to consider developments in these three modalities, despite their emerging nature within the community. In an effort to find language that expresses the emergence of institutions and worldviews before they become fixed and available for classification, Raymond Williams proposed the idea of "structures of feeling" to refer to meanings and values that change as people live before categories and institutions become definable in time (1977, 131–32). I would suggest that, in the case of this refugee population, Somali Bantu cultural identity and adolescence are two such structures of feeling, while gender remains the least changeable within the experience of dislocation.

Cultural Identity

As I noted earlier, the identifier *Somali Bantu* is a relatively new phenomenon, one that was invented by early twentieth-century Italian ethnographers to differentiate one population in Somalia from the more dominant ethnic group, and which was then adopted within the camps by international refugee organizations for the same purpose. In lived practice among this specific community of refugees at Wedgewood, members of the Somali Bantu population are made up of at least two ethnic groups speaking distinct languages. Yet this emerging, overarching Somali Bantu identity operates meaningfully alongside that of Zigua and Maay-maay. At this moment in their history, the members of the community recognize both levels of identity: an ethnolinguistic one, and another supra-ethnic one, based on shared history and marginalization in Somalia, and flight and resettlement outside it. It is important to note that one identity has not supplanted the other; rather, Somali Bantuness is a structure of feeling that is emerging out of the crisis of the last two decades and prior history. It is not yet fixed but nevertheless of importance to the group. It remains to be seen, as young people in this community integrate more thoroughly into U.S. life, and the various ethnic factions access the technology to preserve the specifics of their expressive culture, whether both ethnic and supra-ethnic identifiers will remain meaningful, and to what extent an American identity will emerge within the group.

As a differential identity, however, the idea of Somali Bantuness remains contested by the dominant Somali ethnic group. In one of my early forays into research within this population, I attended a 2007 Somali Studies conference at the Ohio State University. In the midst of a lecture by Omar Eno, a prominent Somali Bantu scholar and advocate, ethnic Somalis within the audience began to challenge him about the need for this population to identify themselves as separate from other Somali refugees. Tempers escalated quickly, as many of the ethnic Somalis clearly resented the distinctions made by the minority group, and Eno defended their separate history and background vociferously, as he has done in other venues (1997). This spirited exchange within an academic context, which was unresolved, echoes throughout the larger diasporic Somali community. Ethnic Somali teachers and administrators with the Municipal Schools routinely expressed their discomfort with my research project, because it lent credibility to an identity claim they find illegitimate. This, in turn, was paradoxical since they repeatedly indicated that the Bantu were different from (and generally inferior to) them when pressed into discussion. In some instances, these interactions indicated a degree of hostility that went beyond mere academic distinctions. In contrast, during my conversations with adult members of the Somali Bantu community, the claim of Somali Bantu identity as culturally and historically distinct from the ethnic Somalis was made with deep feeling. Somali Bantuness operates as a significant element of identity at this point in the historical circumstances of state collapse and dislocation. In her extensive study of the emergence of Hutu and Tutsi identity within refugee camps, Liisa Malkki (1995) argues that the refugee experience, in certain instances, is normative for cultural identity, despite the perception that refugees are stripped of cultural elements when they are dislocated into camps. Rather than in the stability of home, she notes, it is in the camps where a group mythico-history circulates in oral narrative, the characteristics of the ethnic other are cemented (whether of enemies before flight or those found within the camps), physical differences along ethnic lines are reinforced, and tales of victimization become increasingly important within group history.

While Malkki concentrates on stories that circulate within Hutu communities, narrative forms of expressive culture are not the sole means of reinforcing an emerging cultural identity. This project has relied on aesthetic, entertainment, consumer, ritual, and video circulation practices as texts (Geertz 1972) that can be read in the ongoing construction of cultural identity among the Somali Bantu. In this instance, even as expressive forms as central to identity formation as initiation ritual are disrupted, the practice of expressive culture remains "the principal means by which an individual and a group discovers or establishes his or its identity" (Dundes 1989, 35). Somali Bantu cultural identity continues to develop and establish itself in housing projects across the American landscape, but how will it evolve as its youngest members move more deeply into American life? Will the differential identity that has served to undergird the supra-ethnic identity remain significant without a dominant ethnic

Somali community to define it against? It is impossible to answer these questions in the short term; at this moment, it remains an important element of identity even as it emerges in practice.

Life Cycle Status

In an insightful review of anthropological literature on adolescence, Mary Bucholtz points out that, thanks in part to a focus on initiation rituals by ethnographers, adolescence has largely been regarded as a liminal phase among scholars, a way station on the path to adulthood and full enculturation in society. This approach emphasizes the role of adults in guiding socialization, but it obscures the ways young people socialize themselves and one another. In fact, she notes, for young people, youth is often an identity, not a trajectory (2002, 529–32), and as such, it "is agentive, flexible, and ever-changing—but no more for youth than for people of any age" (2002, 532). The teenagers who were part of my study seem to be caught between two approaches to the life cycle. In many respects, these young people participate in their community as uninitiated members, living in the homes of their mothers regardless of gender, remaining dependent on their elders, and often contributing to the household labor as subordinates. They recognize that their existence is part of a trajectory, not an end unto itself, and that vision actually prevents a great deal of frustration with their role as pre-adults. James Coté has noted that the use of puberty rites to separate childhood from adulthood proliferates within groups that need labor from their young, so they create a clear line of demarcation (Coté and Allahar 1996, 70). That need remains within the Somali Bantu community, and the teenagers who were part of this study recognized that their move into adulthood depended on becoming independent economic agents. The categories of child and adult, with their well-maintained boundaries, remain in effect.

On the other hand, a practice of adolescence is emerging within their generation, and it is influenced by the surrounding U.S. context. Through participation in high school, these teens are integrated with members of other cultural groups, and an identity based on extended experience in school and its rituals of development is growing. Their exposure to multiple forms of media allows them to integrate elements of Nollywood, hip-hop culture, sports competitions, and consumer goods into this emerging practice of adolescence. Coté has noted that, in industrial societies, young people are more symbol oriented, so they define themselves by how they look, making statements through clothing, hairstyles, and cosmetics (Coté and Allahar 1996, 81). This trend is also growing within this generation of refugees and can be seen in circulated cell-phone photos, aesthetic demands during wedding rituals, and increased fluency in hip-hop culture. Despite their subordinate position within the housing project, they are pioneers within their community, inventing a new identity as adolescents through everyday practice.

By and large, these young people have a foot in both identities. At school, and within peer groups, they act like adolescents. They circulate secrets of girlfriends and boyfriends, compete at sports and studies, and imitate practices of the American teen life that surrounds them. At home, they fade into background roles as expected and look for ways to move into adulthood, whether through the offer of marriage by a Somali Bantu male with the required means or through employment that will provide the means to offer marriage. Adolescence is not yet an identity in this group, but it—like Somali Bantuness—is emerging steadily in everyday life. Only long-term longitudinal research will illustrate how this first Somali Bantu peer group to experience adolescence develops as adults, how the stage of adolescence evolves as increasingly Americanized young Somali Bantu refugees mature into it, and whether there will be a place for the continued practice of initiation rituals.

Gender

While the experience of dislocation and resettlement has created considerable flux in the construction of identity among the Somali Bantu, gender remains the aspect of identity most resistant to disruption, remaining a central "container of meaning" of considerable importance regardless of location (Abrahams 2003, 217). Not only does it dominate how life is organized in the community but, for young people, it also continues to shape how they operate in daily life and how they perceive their options for adulthood, regardless of how far they are removed from the structuring experiences of their parents. Mary Douglas has noted that rituals enact social relations and, by giving those social relations visible expression in ritual, people understand their own society. In any group, rituals work on the body politic through the symbolic medium of the physical body ([1966] 2002, 128). In the case of the Somali Bantu, even in the midst of considerable disruption in ritual practice, the practice that directly constructs gender identity on an individual within the group is the element of initiation ritual that remained significant for the Somali Bantu. It is clear that both this physical construction and the social reality it symbolizes are fundamental within this community.

What is less clear is how meaningful either aspect will remain as young Somali Bantu teenagers become increasingly integrated into U.S. life. The question of gender in diaspora is one that needs considerable future study, as it has served to be the most conservative modality of identity in this initial period of resettlement, but as noted in the research on genital cutting in diaspora, it is changing even as marriageability remains critical for young women (Johansen 2007; Johnsdotter 2007; Talle 2007). Only future research will indicate if its force is largely because of the physical modification of genitalia that constructs gender, how long-term resettlement in the United States will affect the anatomical aspects of initiation practices, and whether gender will remain a socially conservative force.

Identity in Crisis

Earlier in the book, I discussed the notion of identity postulated by Erik Erikson (1959) in which identity is formed as individuals struggle to overcome obstacles and meet their own desires in culturally appropriate ways. The sense of continuity that they develop as individuals over time and in different social situations provides ego identity, while sociocultural surroundings provide guidance and support to mitigate the stress of development. In a similar vein, then, cultural identity is also a sense of continuity that develops over time within a community. I further noted in the introduction that this period of time within the cultural history of the Somali Bantu is one of identity crisis as both the sense of continuity over time of the groups that make up the Somali Bantu community and the ritual practice of initiation have been disrupted by the experience of flight and resettlement. Despite the crisis, the community has responded creatively, constructing a Somali Bantu aesthetic identity based on assemblage while reinforcing the role of gender as it is constructed in traditional ritual practice, blending elements of American and African media to reinforce gender roles within the American context, adopting new ritual practices from the American school system, and adapting traditional wedding practices to reinforce the traditional responsibilities of adulthood.

Put simply, the Somali Bantu community has responded to the identity crisis of resettlement through adaptation of form and reinforcement of life cycle and gender roles. In a vivid way, they have reconciled the two poles of identity construction noted by Stuart Hall earlier in this book. Somali Bantu identity is in the process of becoming, while it also relies on certain unchanged frames of reference and meaning within the disruptions of the preceding two decades of their history (S. Hall 2003, 234–36). What is currently impossible to predict is how stable it will remain if the gender roles inculcated traditionally by initiation ritual and reinforced in practice within the community eventually destabilize.

Passage Forward

This book has attempted to illustrate the indigenous solutions of the Somali Bantu community in the midst of a multilayered identity crisis brought on by dislocation and resettlement, but it has been limited in scope and time. As this resettlement continues across the United States, and the young people whose experience of life has been shaped by refugee camps and housing projects approach adulthood, the Somali Bantu will continue to shape group values into meaningful form. In the meantime, these teenagers move about in a dizzying blur of expectations. As at the skating rink I described at the start of this work, the noise of the surrounding culture limits their ability to hear and follow the directions aimed to prevent them from crashing into others and causing harm to themselves. Demonstrating more fluency in the surrounding culture, the teenage boys whirl past tripping girls, only to find themselves in a perpetual circle of noise and lights while the girls support one another and move to safety. Yet the same girls, over time and with the shedding of layers of traditional garments, reveal a similar competence in the surrounding American culture, and slowly achieve success on their skates. Like the rink, the experience of dislocation and resettlement remains dizzying and uncertain for these teenagers, and provides an uncertain destination. Yet they continue to move forward.

Afterword

From Adolescence into Adulthood

Some five and a half years after my last visit to Linmoor, I found myself back at a Wedgewood wedding, this time Tahlil's. The tall, level-headed young man with considerable natural leadership skills who first appeared in chapter 1 recently married a young woman from the community, and they celebrated in style. While the guests danced to Somali disco music, the bride changed from a white wedding dress into a stylish version of traditional African dress, then into a final conservative costume that, if anything, resembled Indian dress. The community celebrated by showering the couple with coins and small bills, while their escorts danced throughout the reception.

Although my regular visits to the estate had also come to an end, over the years I have remained in contact with Tahlil and many of the young people I met in this research. When I have the opportunity to visit Wedgewood, I still come and go from Abuukar and Basra's apartment, catching up on the news of their family and the larger Somali Bantu community in the area. Aasiya, who provided guidance to me about being a good wife in chapter 3, finally got a chance to exercise her skills at it when her husband received an entry visa and moved to Wedgewood. In addition to the little girl they had together in East Africa, they now have a young son born in the United States. Abuukar and Basra remain ensconced at Wedgewood as their family grows. Basra's apartment is still a haven for the myriad of grandchildren who live within the housing estate. Over the years, the cloths on her walls and ceilings have demonstrated increasing wealth and style, and the apartment remains a hub of activity. Abuukar continues to work at FedEx, but their grandson Mahdi noted to me that he hopes his grandfather will retire soon and enjoy his later years, as he is starting to tire from the hard work and struggles over the course of his lifetime.

The teenagers I knew have progressed into their twenties, and as they have matured, patterns have emerged in the choices they make about Somali Bantu adulthood in diaspora. As expected, most of the girls followed Timiro's lead, and were married during or soon after their time at Linmoor. At the time of Tahlil's wedding, nearly all of the girls whom I had known in this research were married and had begun to establish families, some at Wedgewood and others in Somali Bantu enclaves in other cities. Maryan, whose struggles to find a husband were detailed in chapter 6, married shortly after she finished at Linmoor and moved to a Somali Bantu community about three hours from her family, near her friend Timiro. She has recently delivered a second child. Timiro, whose wedding was detailed in chapter 6, remains married with three children, but has moved away to Omaha with her husband and family. Dahabo married while still in school, and she currently has four or five children. That marriage has experienced some difficulties; at one point her husband left her at Wedgewood and moved to Arizona to start a family with another woman. At last report, he had moved back to the Midwest and the family he started with Dahabo. Haajiro, one of the youngest girls I encountered in fieldwork, finished high school, married, and moved to Milwaukee to be with her husband. They have one child. Mako remains at Wedgewood, where she is married and has become very religious; she reportedly spends considerable time at the local mosque and works as a teacher in its school. Among the age group who were the focus of my research, the sole exception to this ubiquitous pattern is Hagarla, who, at the time of this writing, was not yet married but was working as a cleaner and planning for a wedding in the coming year. What is currently unknown is if this pattern has remained consistent among those young women who were part of the U.S. school system from a younger age; further study is needed on both sets of young refugees.

While almost all of the girls in this study have already secured their future through the establishment of families, the boys—now in their early twenties— are currently in the midst of establishing themselves. The week before Tahlil's wedding, his cousin Heybe also got married to the mother of his child. Both young men have fairly stable jobs; Tahlil is working in construction and Heybe in a warehouse. I noted in chapter 1 that there had been considerable concern about Heybe, given his flashes of anger and close friendship with those attempting to form a Somali Bantu gang. Both Tahlil and Mahdi report that he has matured into a happy man and caring father. Among their agemates, many remain unmarried while they position themselves as providers for a family. Mahdi, the grandson of Abuukar and Basra, is completing a program in medical coding and, while he eyes potential wives both in the United States and East Africa, he plans to delay any marriage until he has finished school. Haaruun is currently working and attempting to raise the six to eight thousand dollars he

needs to contract a desired marriage. Obsiye, who appeared in the introduction, moved to a neighboring state to pursue school, but returned to the area
and works for FedEx. He is not yet married. Unfortunately, not all the young
men in this study are finding legitimate employment or forming stable relationships in the community as they mature into adulthood. Ibraahin, the young
man in chapter 3 who was trying to decide between finishing school and learning
a trade, appears to have chosen neither. After leaving Linmoor for the local
mainstream high school, Ibraahin became involved in drinking and smoking
marijuana. He was reportedly arrested in Colorado for selling drugs, but has
moved back to Wedgewood. Likewise, Hanad, the champion arm wrestler
from chapter 3, also has become involved in drinking and smoking marijuana
after fathering a child and considering—then passing up—a stint in the U.S.
military; following two reported incarcerations, he lives with American friends
outside the Somali Bantu community.

Marriages and babies are easier to verify than official progress in education.
All of the students who appeared in this work have finished school in some
fashion. However, what I could not verify is whether all the students graduated
from the Municipal Schools and successfully completed the State Graduation
Test. Clearly a few, like Mahdi, have continued in their studies, which would
require them to accomplish both. Most have settled into jobs requiring heavy
labor. It is difficult to verify how many of the teens who had landed directly in
high school from refugee camps in Kenya were able to clear all the hurdles in
the school system that are necessary for further study. Seemingly, even for
those who seemed to complete every requirement successfully, the pull to establish a family has been greater than the pull toward pursuing further education.
Tahlil, for example, who once considered a career in law enforcement, seems
content to remain in construction. Hagarla once discussed the possibility of
studying nursing, but works as a cleaner. Within their peer group, they are considered successful, as their stable income allows them the means to establish
families. With so many members of the community co-located in various housing
projects, the young people are generally content to remain there as well. Further
study will be needed to determine how these young people—and the age
groups that follow them—develop in their lives, families, education, and careers.

Works Cited

Abdalla, Raqiya Haji Dualeh. 1982. *Sisters in Affliction: Circumcision and Infibulation of Women in Africa*. London: Zed Press.

Abrahams, Roger. 2003. "Identity." In *Eight Words for the Study of Expressive Culture*, edited by Burt Feintuch, 198–222. Urbana: University of Illinois Press.

Abu-Lughod, Lila. 1997. "The Interpretation of Culture(s) after Television." *Representations* 59:109–34.

Adiele, Faith, and Mary Frosch. 2007. *Coming of Age around the World: A Multicultural Anthology*. New York: Free Press.

Affi, Ladan. 2004. "Domestic Conflict in the Diaspora-Somali Women Asylum Seekers and Refugees in Canada." In *Somalia—the Untold Story: The War through the Eyes of Somali Women*, edited by Judith Gardner and Judy El-Bushra, 107–15. London: Catholic Institute for International Relations.

African Rights. 1993. *The Nightmare Continues . . . : Abuses against Somali Refugees in Kenya*. London: African Rights.

Ahmadu, Fuambai. 2000. "Rites and Wrongs: An Insider/Outsider Reflects on Power and Excision." In *Female "Circumcision" in Africa: Culture, Controversy, and Change*, edited by Bettina Shell-Duncan and Ylva Hernlund, 283–312. Boulder, CO: Lynne Rienner Publishers.

———. 2007. "'Ain't I a Woman Too?'" In *Transcultural Bodies: Female Genital Cutting in Global Context*, edited by Bettina Shell-Duncan and Ylva Hernlund, 278–310. New Brunswick, NJ: Rutgers University Press.

Allen, James de Vere. 1993. *Swahili Origins: Swahili Culture and the Shungwaya Phenomenon*. Athens: Ohio University Press.

Amit-Talai, Vered, and Helena Wulff. 1995. *Youth Cultures: A Cross Cultural Perspective*. London: Routledge.

Appadurai, Arjun. 1996. *Modernity at Large: Cultural Dimensions of Globalization*. Minneapolis: University of Minnesota Press.

Ariès, Philippe. 1962. *Centuries of Childhood: a Social History of Family Life*. New York: Vintage Books.

Bakan, David. (1971) 1972. "Adolescence in America: From Idea to Social Fact." In *Twelve to Sixteen: Early Adolescence*, edited by Jerome and Robert Coles Kagan, 75–89. New York: W. W. Norton.

Ball, Michael R. 1990. *Professional Wrestling as Ritual Drama in American Popular Culture.* Lewiston, NY: Edwin Mellen Press.

Barth, Fredrik. 1969. *Ethnic Groups and Boundaries: The Social Organization of Culture Difference.* Boston: Little, Brown.

Basso, Keith H. 1996. "Wisdom Sits in Places: Notes on a Western Apache Landscape." In *Senses of Place*, edited by Steven Feld and Keith H. Basso, 53–90. Santa Fe, NM: School of American Research Press.

Bauman, Richard. 1971. "Differential Identity and the Social Base of Folklore." *Journal of American Folklore* 84, no. 331: 31–41.

Bausinger, Hermann. 1990. *Folk Culture in a World of Technology.* Bloomington: Indiana University Press.

Beidelman, T. O. 1991. "Containing Time: Rites of Passage and Moral Space or Bachelard among the Kaguru, 1957–1966." *Anthropos* 86:443–61.

Berman, Bruce, and John Lonsdale. 1992. *Unhappy Valley: Conflict in Kenya and Africa.* Bk. 2, *Violence and Ethnicity.* Eastern African Studies 2. London: J. Currey.

Berns-McGown, Rima. 1999. *Muslims in the Diaspora: The Somali Communities of London and Toronto.* Toronto: University of Toronto Press.

Besteman, Catherine Lowe. 1995. "The Invention of Gosha: Slavery, Colonialism, and Stigma in Somali History." In *The Invention of Somalia*, edited by Ali Jimale Ahmed, 43–62. Lawrenceville, NJ: Red Sea Press.

———. 1999. *Unraveling Somalia: Race, Violence, and the Legacy of Slavery.* Philadelphia: University of Pennsylvania Press.

Besteman, Catherine Lowe, and Lee V. Cassanelli. 2000. *The Struggle for Land in Southern Somalia: The War behind the War.* London: Haan.

Blum, Ernst. 1926. "The Psychology of Study and Examinations." *International Journal of Psychoanalysis* 7:457–69.

Boddy, Janice Patricia. 1982. "Womb as Oasis: The Symbolic Context of Pharaonic Circumcision in Rural Northern Sudan." *American Ethnologist* 9, no. 4: 682–98.

———. 1989. *Wombs and Alien Spirits: Women, Men, and the Zar Cult in Northern Sudan.* New Directions in Anthropological Writing. Madison: University of Wisconsin Press.

———. 2007. "Gender Crusades: The Female Circumcision Controversy in Cultural Perspective." In *Transcultural Bodies: Female Genital Cutting in Global Context*, edited by Bettina Shell-Duncan and Ylva Hernlund, 46–66. New Brunswick, NJ: Rutgers University Press.

Bourdieu, Pierre. (1982) 1992. "Rites as Acts of Institution." In *Honor and Grace in Anthropology*, edited by John G. and Julian Alfred Pitt-Rivers Peristiany, 79–89. Cambridge: Cambridge University Press.

Bronner, Simon J. 2006. *Crossing the Line: Violence, Play, and Drama in Naval Equator Traditions.* Amsterdam: Amsterdam University Press.

Bucholtz, Mary. 2002. "Youth and Cultural Practice." *Annual Review of Anthropology* 31:525–52.

Burton, Richard Francis. 1872. *Zanzibar: City, Island, and Coast*. London: Tinsley.

CAHS. n.d. "About Us." http://cahs.ccsoh.us/AboutUs.aspx. Accessed March 1, 2009.

Cassanelli, Lee V. 1988. "The End of Slavery and the 'Problem' of Farm Labor in Colonial Somalia." In *Proceedings of the Third International Congress of Somali Studies*, edited by Annarita Puglielli, 269–82. Rome: Pensiero scientifico editore.

———. 1989. "Social Construction on the Somali Frontier: Bantu Former Slave Communities in the Nineteenth Century." In *The African Frontier: The Reproduction of Traditional African Societies*, edited by Igor Kopytoff, 216–38. Bloomington: Indiana University Press.

CCS. n.d. "Program Description for the HS Welcome Center." http://www.columbus .k12.oh.us/hswelcomecenter/pro_descript.html. Accessed March 7, 2009.

Certeau, Michel de. 1984. *The Practice of Everyday Life*. Berkeley: University of California Press.

Cerulli, Enrico. 1957. *Somalia: Scritti vari editi ed inediti*. 2 vols. Rome: Istituto poligrafico dello Stato P.V.

Chikere, Tchidi, dir. 2007. *Stronger than Pain*. Nigeria: O. Gabby Innovations, Ltd.

Clair, Jeffrey M., David Allen Karp, and William C. Yoels. 1993. *Experiencing the Life Cycle: A Social Psychology of Aging*. 2nd ed. Springfield, IL: C. C. Thomas.

Cooper, Frederick. 1997. *Plantation Slavery on the East Coast of Africa*. Portsmouth, NH: Heinemann.

Coté, James E. 2000. *Arrested Adulthood: The Changing Nature of Maturity and Identity*. New York: New York University Press.

Coté, James E., and Anton Allahar. 1996. *Generation on Hold: Coming of Age in the Late Twentieth Century*. New York: New York University Press.

Custodio, Brenda. 2009. "The Effects of the No Child Left Behind Act on Newcomer Programs." In "How to Design and Implement a Newcomer Program." Unpublished manuscript. Columbus, Ohio.

Davis, Natalie Zemon. 1975. "Women on Top." In *Society and Culture in Early Modern France: Eight Essays*, 124–51. Stanford: Stanford University Press.

Declich, Francesca. 1995a. "'Gendered Narratives,' History, and Identity: Two Centuries along the Juba River among the Zigula and Shanbara." *History in Africa*, no. 22: 191–222.

———. 1995b. "Identity, Dance, and Islam among People with Bantu Origins in Riverine Areas of Somalia." In *The Invention of Somalia*, edited by Ali Jimale Ahmed, xv, 93–122. Lawrenceville, NJ: Red Sea Press.

———. 2000. "Fostering Ethnic Reinvention: Gender Impact of Forced Migration on Bantu Somali Refugees in Kenya." *Cahiers d'etudes africaines*, no. 157:25–53.

Dopico, Mansura. 2007. "Infibulation and the Orgasm Puzzle." In *Transcultural Bodies: Female Genital Cutting in Global Context*, edited by Bettina Shell-Duncan and Ylva Hernlund, 224–47. New Brunswick, NJ: Rutgers University Press.

Dorkenoo, Efua. 1994. *Cutting the Rose: Female Genital Mutilation: The Practice and Its Prevention.* Minority Rights Publications. London: Minority Rights Group.

Douglas, Mary. (1966) 2002. *Purity and Danger: An Analysis of Concept of Pollution and Taboo.* London: Routledge.

Dundes, Alan. 1989. "Defining Identity through Folklore." In *Folklore Matters*, 1–39. Knoxville: University of Tennessee Press.

Eliade, Mircea. 1965. *Rites and Symbols of Initiation: The Mysteries of Birth and Rebirth.* New York: Harper and Row.

Ellis, Bill. (1991) 1996. "Legend-Trips and Satanism: Adolescents' Ostensive Traditions as 'Cult' Activity." In *Contemporary Legend: A Reader*, edited by Gillian Bennett and Paul Smith, 167–86. New York: Garland Pub.

Eno, Omar. 1997. "The Untold Apartheid Imposed on the Bantu/Jarer People in Somalia." In *Mending Rips in the Sky: Options for Somali Communities in the 21st Century*, edited by Hussein Mohammed Adam and Richard B. Ford, 209–20. Lawrenceville, NJ: Red Sea Press.

Erikson, Erik H. 1959. *Identity and the Life Cycle: Selected Papers.* New York: International Universities Press.

Fair, Laura. 1998. "Dressing Up: Clothing, Class, and Gender in Post-Abolition Zanzibar." *Journal of African History* 39:63–94.

Fine, Gary Alan. 1987. *With the Boys: Little League Baseball and Preadolescent Culture.* Chicago: University of Chicago Press.

Foley, Douglas E. 1990. *Learning Capitalist Culture: Deep in the Heart of Tejas.* Contemporary Ethnography Series. Philadelphia: University of Pennsylvania Press.

Freud, Sigmund, James Strachey, and Anna Freud. (1905) 1953. "Three Essays on Sexuality." In *The Standard Edition of the Complete Psychological Works of Sigmund Freud*, 125–248. London: Hogarth Press.

Frosch, Mary. 1994. *Coming of Age in America: A Multicultural Anthology.* New York: New Press.

Geertz, Clifford. 1972. "Deep Play: Notes on the Balinese Cockfight." *Daedalus* 101, no. 1: 1–37.

Gele, Abdi A., Bernadette Kumar, Karin Harslof Hjelde, and Johannes Sundby. 2012. "Attitudes toward Female Circumcision among Somali Immigrants in Oslo: A Qualitative Study." *International Journal of Women's Health* 4:7–17.

Giroux, Henry A. 1983. *Theory and Resistance in Education: A Pedagogy for the Opposition.* South Hadley, MA: Bergin and Garvey Publishers.

Goffman, Erving. 1959. *The Presentation of Self in Everyday Life.* Garden City, NY: Doubleday.

Gow, Greg. 2002. *The Oromo in Exile: From the Horn of Africa to the Suburbs of Australia.* Carlton: Melbourne University Press.

Grimes, Ronald L. 2000. *Deeply into the Bone: Re-Inventing Rites of Passage.* Berkeley: University of California Press.

Grottanelli, V. L. 1955. *Pescatori del Oceano Indiano.* Rome: Cremonese.

Guillain, M. 1856. *Documents sur l'Histoire, la Géographie, et le Commerce de L'Afrique Orientale.* Edited by Arthus Bertrand. Vol. 2. Paris: Libraire de la Société de Géographie.

Habermas, Jürgen. 1984. *The Theory of Communicative Action.* Vol. 1. Boston: Beacon Press.

Hall, G. Stanley. 1904. *Adolescence: Its Psychology and Its Relations to Physiology, Anthropology, Sociology, Sex, Crime, Religion and Education.* New York: D. Appleton.

Hall, Kathleen. 2002. *Lives in Translation: Sikh Youth as British Citizens.* Philadelphia: University of Pennsylvania Press.

Hall, Stuart. 2003. "Cultural Identity and Diaspora." In *Theorizing Diaspora: A Reader,* edited by Jana Evans Braziel and Anita Mannur, 233–46. Malden, MA: Blackwell.

Hannerz, Ulf. 1989. "Notes on the Global Ecumene." *Public Culture* 1:66–75.

Hansen, Karen Tranberg. 2010. "Secondhand Clothing and Fashion in Africa." In *Contemporary African Fashion,* edited by Suzanne and Kristyne Loughran Gott, 39–51. Bloomington: Indiana University Press.

Harding, Frances. 2003. "Africa and the Moving Image: Television, Film and Video." *Journal of African Cultural Studies* 16, no. 1: 69–84.

Harris, Marvin. 1988. *Culture, People, Nature: an Introduction to General Anthropology.* 5th ed. New York: HarperCollins.

Haynes, Jonathan. 2000. Introduction to *Nigerian Video Films,* edited by J. Haynes, 1–36. Athens: Ohio University Center for International Studies.

Hernlund, Ylva, and Bettina Shell-Duncan. 2007. "Transcultural Positions: Negotiating Rights and Culture." In *Transcultural Bodies: Female Genital Cutting in Global Context,* edited by Bettina Shell-Duncan and Ylva Hernlund, 1–45. New Brunswick, NJ: Rutgers University Press.

HIV/AIDS, World Health Organization and Joint United Nations Programme on. 2007. *Male Circumcision: Global Trends and Determinants of Prevalence, Safety and Acceptability.* Geneva, Switzerland: World Health Organization.

Jenkins, Henry. 1997. "'Never Trust a Snake': WWF Wrestling as Masculine Melodrama." In *Out of Bounds: Sports, Media, and the Politics of Identity,* edited by Aaron Baker and Todd Boyd, 48–78. Bloomington: Indiana University Press.

Johansen, R. Elise B. 2007. "Experiencing Sex in Exile: Can Genitals Change Their Gender?" In *Transcultural Bodies: Female Genital Cutting in Global Context,* edited by Bettina Shell-Duncan and Ylva Hernlund, 248–77. New Brunswick, NJ: Rutgers University Press.

Johnsdotter, Sara. 2007. "Persistence of Tradition or Reassessment of Cultural Practices in Exile? Discourses on Female Circumcision among and about Swedish Somalis." In *Transcultural Bodies: Female Genital Cutting in Global Context,* edited by Bettina Shell-Duncan and Ylva Hernlund, 107–34. New Brunswick, NJ: Rutgers University Press.

Jones, Michael Owen, Michael Dane Moore, and Richard Christopher Snyder. 1988. *Inside Organizations: Understanding the Human Dimension.* Newbury Park, CA: Sage Publications.

Kapchan, Deborah. 1993. "Moroccan Women's Body Signs." In *Bodylore,* edited by Katharine Galloway Young, 3–34. Knoxville: University of Tennessee Press.

Kett, Joseph F. 1977. *Rites of Passage: Adolescence in America, 1790 to the Present.* New York: Basic Books.

Kiell, Norman. 1964. *The Universal Experience of Adolescence.* New York: International Universities Press.

Kirshenblatt-Gimblett, Barbara. 1983. "The Future of Folklore Studies in America: The Urban Frontier." *Folklore Forum* 16:175–234.

Krapf, J. L., and Ernest George Ravenstein. 1860. *Travels, Researches, and Missionary Labors during an Eighteen Years' Residence in Eastern Africa: Together with Journeys to Jagga, Usambara, Ukambani, Shoa, Abessinia and Khartum, and a Coasting Voyage from Mombaz to Cape Delgado.* Boston: Ticknor and Fields.

Kratz, Corinne A. 2007. "Seeking Asylum, Debating Values, and Setting Precedents in the 1990s: The Cases of Kassindja and Abankwah in the United States." In *Transcultural Bodies: Female Genital Cutting in Global Context,* edited by Bettina Shell-Duncan and Ylva Hernlund, 167–201. New Brunswick, NJ: Rutgers University Press.

Kusow, Abdi M. 1995. "The Somali Origin: Myth or Reality." In *The Invention of Somalia,* edited by Ali Jimale Ahmed, 81–106. Lawrenceville, NJ: Red Sea Press.

Lancy, David F. 1996. *Playing on the Mother-Ground: Cultural Routines for Children's Development, Culture and Human Development.* New York: Guilford Press.

Langlois, Janet L. 1985. "Belle Gunness, the Lady Bluebeard: Narrative Use of a Deviant Woman." In *Women's Folklore, Women's Culture,* edited by R. A. Jordan and Susan Kalčik, 109–25. Philadelphia: University of Pennsylvania Press.

Larkin, Brian. 1997. "Indian Films and Nigerian Lovers: Media and the Creation of Parallel Modernities." *Africa: Journal of the International African Institute* 67, no. 3: 406–40.

Leemon, Thomas. 1972. *The Rites of Passage in a Student Culture: A Study of the Dynamics of Transition.* New York: Teachers College Press, Columbia University.

Lightfoot-Klein, Hanny. 1989. *Prisoners of Ritual: An Odyssey into Female Genital Circumcision in Africa.* New York: Haworth Press.

Luling, Virginia. 1971. "The Social Structure of the Southern Somali Tribes." PhD diss., University of London.

———. 2002. *Somali Sultanate: The Geledi City-State over 150 Years.* Piscataway, NJ: Transaction Publishers.

Lyons, Harriet D. 2007. "Genital Cutting: The Past and Present of a Polythetic Category." *Africa Today* 53, no. 4: 3–17.

Mahdi, Louise Carus, Nancy Geyer Christopher, and Michael Meade. 1996. *Crossroads: The Quest for Contemporary Rites of Passage.* Chicago: Open Court.

Mahdi, Louise Carus, Steven Foster, and Meredith Little. 1987. *Betwixt and Between: Patterns of Masculine and Feminine Initiation.* La Salle, IL: Open Court.

Maira, Sunaina, and Elisabeth Soep. 2005. *Youthscapes: The Popular, the National, the Global.* Philadelphia: University of Pennsylvania Press.

Malkki, Liisa H. 1995. *Purity and Exile: Violence, Memory, and National Cosmology among Hutu Refugees in Tanzania.* Chicago: University of Chicago Press.

Masao, F. T., and H. W. Mutoro. 1988. "The East African Coast and the Comoro Islands." In *Africa from the Seventh to the Eleventh Century*, edited by Muhammad El Fasi and Ivan Hrbek, 586–615. London: Heinemann Educational Books.

Matan, Abdulkadir. 2007. Interview. Grove City, Ohio, January 20.

Mazer, Sharon. 1998. *Professional Wrestling: Sport and Spectacle*. Jackson: University Press of Mississippi.

McCall, John C. 2002. "Madness, Money, and Movies: Watching a Nigerian Popular Video with the Guidance of a Native Doctor." *Africa Today* 49, no. 3: 79–94.

McDermott, John J. 1987. "Deprivation and Celebration: Suggestions for an Aesthetic Ecology." In *The Culture of Experience: Philosophical Essays in the American Grain*, 82–98. Prospect Heights, IL: Waveland Press.

McLaren, Peter. 1994. *Life in Schools: An Introduction to Critical Pedagogy in the Foundations of Education*. New York: Longman.

McMahon, Felicia R. 2007. *Not Just Child's Play: Emerging Tradition and the Lost Boys of Sudan*. Jackson: University Press of Mississippi.

Mead, Margaret. (1928) 1961. *Coming of Age in Samoa: A Psychological Study of Primitive Youth for Western Civilization*. New York: William Morrow.

Menken, Kate. 2008. *English Learners Left Behind: Standardized Testing as Language Policy*. Edited by Nancy H. and Colin Baker Hornberger. Bilingual Education and Bilingualism 65. Clevedon: Multilingual Matters.

Menkhaus, Kenneth. 1989. "Rural Transformation and the Roots of Underdevelopment in Somalia's Lower Jubba Valley." PhD diss., University of South Carolina.

Moffatt, Michael. 1989. *Coming of Age in New Jersey: College and American Culture*. New Brunswick, NJ: Rutgers University Press.

Moore, Sally Falk, and Barbara G. Myerhoff. 1977. *Secular Ritual*. Assen: Van Gorcum.

Morton, R. F. 1972. "The Shungwaya Myth of Miji Kenda Origins: A Problem of Late Nineteenth-Century Coastal History." *International Journal of African Historical Studies* 5, no. 3: 397–423.

Musse, Fowzia. 2004. "War Crimes against Women and Girls." In *Somalia — The Untold Story: the War through the Eyes of Somali Women*, edited by Judith Gardner and Judy El-Bushra, 69–96. London: Catholic Institute for International Relations.

Muuss, Rolf Eduard Helmut, Eli Velder, and Harriet Porton. (1975) 1996. *Theories of Adolescence*. 6th ed. New York: McGraw-Hill.

Myerhoff, Barbara G. 1982. "Rites of Passage: Process and Paradox." In *Celebration: Studies in Festivity and Ritual*, edited by Victor Witter Turner, 109–35. Washington, DC: Smithsonian Institution Press.

Naficy, Hamid. 1999. "The Making of Exile Cultures: Iranian Television in Los Angeles." In *The Cultural Studies Reader*, edited by S. During, 537–63. London: Routledge.

Namganga, Hanad. 2008. Interview. Columbus, Ohio, March 11.

Nilan, Pam, and Carles Feixa. 2006. *Global Youth? Hybrid Identities, Plural Worlds*. London: Routledge.

Nowrojee, Binaifer, and Dorothy Q. Thomas. 1993. *Seeking Refuge, Finding Terror*. New York: Human Rights Watch, Africa Watch, and Women's Rights Project.

Noyes, Dorothy. 2003. "Group." In *Eight Words for the Study of Expressive Culture*, edited by Burt Feintuch, 7–41. Urbana: University of Illinois Press.

Nurse, Derek, and Thomas Spear. 1985. *The Swahili: Reconstructing the History and Language of an African Society, 800–1500*. Ethnohistory. Philadelphia: University of Pennsylvania Press.

Obermeyer, Carla Makhlouf. 1999. "Female Genital Surgeries: The Known, the Unknown, and the Unknowable." *Medical Anthropology Quarterly* 13, no. 1: 27.

Oring, Elliot. 1993. "Victor Turner, Sigmund Freud, and the Return of the Repressed." *Ethos* 21, no. 3: 273–94.

———. 1994. "The Arts, Artifacts, and Artifices of Identity." *Journal of American Folklore* 107, no. 424: 211–33.

Piot, Charles. 2007. "Representing Africa in the Kasinga Asylum Case." In *Transcultural Bodies: Female Genital Cutting in Global Context*, edited by Bettina Shell-Duncan and Ylva Hernlund, 157–66. New Brunswick, NJ: Rutgers University Press.

Price, David H. 2003. "Outcome-Based Tyranny: Teaching Compliance While Testing like a State." *Anthropological Quarterly* 76, no. 4: 715–30.

Prins, Adriaan Hendrik Johan. 1950. *The Coastal Tribes of the Northeast Bantu*. London.

Prosterman, Leslie Mina. 1995. *Ordinary Life, Festival Days: Aesthetics in the Midwestern County Fair*. Washington, DC: Smithsonian Institution Press.

Ranger, T. O. 1975. *Dance and Society in Eastern Africa, 1890–1970: The Beni Ngoma*. Berkeley: University of California Press.

Raw. 2009. Television program. March 23. World Wrestling Entertainment.

Richards, Audrey Isabel. 1956. *Chisungu: Girls' Initiation Ceremony among the Bemba of Northern Rhodesia*. New York: Grove Press.

Rose, Ava, and James Friedman. 1997. "Television Sports as Mas(s)culine Cult of Distraction." In *Out of Bounds: Sports, Media, and the Politics of Identity*, edited by Aaron Baker and Todd Boyd, 1–15. Bloomington: Indiana University Press.

Schlegel, Alice, and Herbert Barry. 1991. *Adolescence: An Anthropological Inquiry*. New York: Free Press.

Shell-Duncan, Bettina, and Ylva Hernlund. 2000. "Female 'Circumcision' in Africa: Dimensions of the Practice and Debates." In *Female "Circumcision" in Africa: Culture, Controversy, and Change*, edited by Bettina Shell-Duncan and Ylva Hernlund, 1–40. Boulder, CO: Lynne Rienner Publishers.

Shukla, Pravina. 2008. *The Grace of Four Moons: Dress, Adornment, and the Art of the Body in Modern India*. Bloomington: Indiana University Press.

Steffen, Charles G. 2011. *Mutilating Khalid: The Symbolic Politics of Female Genital Cutting*. Trenton, NJ: Red Sea Press.

Stern, Stephen, and John Allan Cicala. 1991. *Creative Ethnicity: Symbols and Strategies of Contemporary Ethnic Life*. Logan: Utah State University Press.

Talle, Aud. 2007. "Female Circumcision in Africa and Beyond: The Anthropology of a Difficult Issue." In *Transcultural Bodies: Female Genital Cutting in Global Context*, edited by Bettina Shell-Duncan and Ylva Hernlund, 91–106. New Brunswick, NJ: Rutgers University Press.

Taylor, Charles. 2004. *Modern Social Imaginaries, Public Planet Books*. Durham, NC: Duke University Press.

Thomas, Lynn M. 2003. *Politics of the Womb: Women, Reproduction, and the State in Kenya*. Berkeley: University of California Press.

Thorne, Barrie. 1993. *Gender Play: Girls and Boys in School*. New Brunswick, NJ: Rutgers University Press.

Tomaselli, Keyan, Arnold Shepperson, and Maureen Eke. 1999. "Towards a Theory of Orality in African Cinema." In *African Cinema: Postcolonial and Feminist Readings*, edited by K. W. Harrow, 45–71. Trenton, NJ: Africa World Press.

Turner, Victor Witter. 1967. *The Forest of Symbols: Aspects of Ndembu Ritual*. Ithaca, NY: Cornell University Press.

———. 1969. *The Ritual Process: Structure and Anti-Structure*. Chicago: Aldine Publishing.

Turton, E. R. 1975. "Bantu, Galla and Somali Migrations in the Horn of Africa: A Reassessment of the Juba/Tana Area." *Journal of African History* 16, no. 4: 519–37.

Valenzuela, Angela, Linda Prieto, and Madlene P. Hamilton. 2007. "Introduction to the Special Issue: No Child Left Behind (NCLB) and Minority Youth: What the Qualitative Evidence Suggests." *Anthropology and Education Quarterly* 38, no. 1: 1–8.

van Gennep, Arnold. (1909) 1960. *The Rites of Passage*. Translated by Monika B. and Gabrielle L. Caffee Vizedom. Chicago: University of Chicago Press.

Van Lehman, Dan, and Omar Eno. 2003. "The Somali Bantu: Their History and Culture." Center for Applied Linguistics, Washington, DC. http://www.cultural orientation.net/learning/populations/other-populations-from-africa.

Walker, Steve. 2007. "State of Ohio's Refugee and Immigrant Populations." Conference paper presented at the Somali Studies International Association 10th Triennial Conference, Ohio State University, August 16–18.

Weule, Karl, and Alice Werner. 1909. *Native Life in East Africa: The Results of an Ethnological Research Expedition*. New York: D. Appleton and Company.

Williams, Raymond. 1977. "Structures of Feeling." In *Marxism and Literature*, 128–35. Oxford: Oxford University Press.

Workman, Mark E. 1977. "Dramaturgical Aspects of Professional Wrestling Matches." *Folklore Forum* 10, no. 1: 14–20.

World Health Organization. 2008. "Eliminating Female Genital Mutilation: An Inter-agency Statement. UNAIDS, UNDP, UNECA, UNESCO, UNFPA, UNHCHR, UNHCR, UNICEF, UNIFEM, WHO." Geneva, Switzerland: World Health Organization.

Zabus, Chantal. 2008. "From 'Cutting without Ritual' to 'Ritual without Cutting': Voice and Remembering the Excised Body in African Texts and Contexts." In *Bodies and Voices: the Force-Field of Representation and Discourse in Colonial and Postcolonial Studies,* edited by Eva Rask Knudsen Marete Falck Borch, Martin Leer, and Bruce Clunies Ross, 45–67. Amsterdam: Rodopi.

Zissman, Sophie. 2005. Phone interview. Columbus, Ohio, February.

Index

Page numbers in italics indicate illustrations.